NOT ONLY THE DARK

NOT ONLY THE DARK

160 poems on the theme of survival

Edited by Jo Field and Nicky Gould

WordAid.org.uk

First published in 2011 for WordAid.org.uk
by Categorical Books
70 Margate Road, Herne Bay, Kent CT6 7BH

For further information about this and other WordAid projects,
please visit www.wordaid.org.uk

To order more copies, please send a cheque for £12 per copy
(including postage & packing) to Categorical Books at the above
address or visit www.wordaid.org.uk

All profits from the sale of this book will benefit ShelterBox
(www.shelterbox.org, registered charity number 1096479)

British cataloguing in publication
A CIP record for this book is available from the British Library

ISBN 978-1-904662-15-0

Production editor Vicky Wilson
Photography Nancy Wilson

Printed in Great Britain by Lightning Source

Following WordAid's hugely successful anthology *Did I Tell You? 131 poems for Children in Need* comes *Not Only The Dark* – 160 poems on the theme of survival, collected and published to raise money for the charity ShelterBox.

ShelterBox is an international disaster-relief charity that specialises in emergency shelter. It responds instantly to earthquake, volcano, hurricane, tsunami or conflict by delivering boxes of aid. The contents of a typical box might include a large tent, a stove, cooking utensils, water purification equipment, mosquito nets, blankets, a toolkit and a children's pack, although each box is tailored to suit its destination. You can find more information at www.shelterbox.org.

As natural disasters inundate the news with almost the same sad regularity as man-made catastrophes, a publication in support of ShelterBox seemed to us an appropriate venture. When the word went out, plenty of people agreed, and we received more than 480 poems which have, with much discussion and a lot of hair-tearing, been whittled down to the 160 gathered here. The work of poets whose names are wonderfully familiar rubs shoulders with that of poets who are simply wonderful, but we wish to convey a multitude of thanks to *everybody* who responded so magnificently to the call, and to warn that WordAid has other projects planned for the future…

The theme of 'survival' turns out to be broad indeed, interpreted in more ways than we believed possible. Here are poems about war, about weather, about growing up and growing old, about despair and cries for help, yes, but also about turtles and lizards, art, prostitutes, music, onions, cities, landscapes and love: the mundane and the extraordinary, the obvious and the obscure all jostling for attention. You will find the reading of the poems a thought-provoking experience in itself, to be enjoyed alongside the knowledge that, by buying this book, you are helping people to *live* who might otherwise exist without hope.

Jo Field and Nicky Gould
November 2011

CONTENTS

Extract from 'Dunstanburgh'

From a hole in the seaward wall, a snail
Stretches its foreparts, eases its tail,

Oozing over the knobbly grain,
Smoothing the stone with its slimy trail.

Its skirts slacken under it. Stretching one eye
To examine a patch of leafy lichen,

It feels its way down a ribbon of silver,
Studded with seashells, ancient mortar,

Fossil of top-shell, cowrie, lime
Sliding under it. Taking its time.

Its slow mouth working, its gluey strings
Trembling in the breeze like skin,

It slithers over root and stalk
And crevice, the sepulchral dark

Hollow of the sea wall, where
The empty shell's reoccupied –

Invisible creatures twitch inside
An alabaster palace, made

In a single movement, from the twist
Of its newel post to its silky lip,

And everything circular starts again.

Katrina Porteous

sure that you, like me, lament the passive trust
in ingenuity which blunts the days that remain.
My role has only ever been to nudge the crust
you float your cities on, or lace the rain
with what you leak into the sky. Do not test
impartial glaciers, or think the seas benign,
when surely you must know even the best
can only swim so long with bellies full of brine.
Something in your optimism would suggest
a mastery of fate, the skill to lower waterlines
or kill the heat; extrapolations say you're dead as dust.

Surely you must long for endless snows, the air
a counterweight to sea, the land free of the plough,
the seaborne cows we took for mermaids or the roar
of mammoths in the tundra. You need somehow
to set aside these minor-scale extinctions and inure
yourself to this; that you were fractionated long ago,
distilled from hydrocarbons at your crude core,
and when compressed and stratified below
the sediments that mass upon you, what endures
will be prospected and extracted over time, to flow
through pumps to drive new industry, somewhere
among the sundry futures that await you now.

Andy Jackson

Groaning mills of phonecall, spinning wire,
purple ears at the loom. End of shift.
Sneering moon of clock hauls us from sunken seats
and the packed foam gasps and gapes. Tide goes out,

computers bleat at the blank beach. Building settles,
prosthetic limb unclipped. Buses lap
at the people-leak, then filled, heave on.
Passenger lights run wet fingers through the night's drapes.

At home in the mirror, peeling off day's static,
green digits dance in the phantom screen.
Curl in a moony sack and dream: town's wires
and pipes as claws clinging, digging into rubble

of cloth factories, blankets of fluff and soot,
rooting for grip in left clogs and lint.
Tarmac tongue spread across cobbles, failed shuttle
still rattles, shakes under cars.

And wake to the lantern sun, knockerupper
doing rounds. Join the teeming river
that winds between blocks, pushing on,
keeping waterwheels turning.

Duncan Hall

Each morning as I round the bend,
the same shock –
                    that flash of river light, the bridge,
the cooling-towers –
                    always that first sight gasp
as if they've been dropped there –

Yet the landscape knows them: a fragment of old stone
moves sideways, and through a tangle of red
the river glitters, the bridge
spins out its turquoise cobweb and there they stand
like a cruet – squat on the flood-plain, lit
apricot, steaming quietly into this end of night.

I've heard there's a place where fish
swim up and down a ladder, mouthing through murk
like cruising angels;
                    where a student strung himself up for days
from a concrete cliff while the canal
sent back his image;
                    where they hand out packages of pills
to every household, in case of leaks.

But here at my open window the field's
rippled with leaves, and blue,
                    the every morning noise
of cock-crow, unidentified shadows finger-flapping across.

   Susan Wicks

One hundred thousand trillion joules
to turn an ice cap into mush
One hundred thousand billion joules
to erase a major Eastern city
A hundred thousand million joules
to run a car to death
One hundred million of the same
for Fire Brigades to reach the kitten
Ten million just to keep
December from cold feet
A hundred thousand joules for a mug
of tea – A hundred joules
for a second's worth of *War and Peace*
Ten to raise a hand – to lift
an average apple to the lips
A single joule to shout the command
Half a joule to pull the trigger
Just one tenth to push the button
Almost zero to have the thought.

Mario Petrucci

THE YEAR OF THE TREE

I carried a tree
through the Underground.

It was hard. At first,
people scarcely noticed me

and the oak I was lugging
along the platforms –

heavier than a suitcase
and difficult to balance.

We threaded through corridors,
changing lines: up and down stairs,

escalators, and for a moment
I imagined everyone on the planet

taking turns
to carry a tree as daily rite.

A few people asked
Why a tree?

I said it was for my own
edification –

a tree always
has something to teach.

      ***

Sharp gusts
whirred through the corridors

rustling the branches
as I hurried on

past the sweepers
picking up rubbish, scraps of paper.

Be sure to take the tree
with you, they said.

Don't worry, I'm taking it
to my garden,

the start of a forest.
When people stared,

Relax, I said,
it's a tree, not a gun.

    Katherine Gallagher

New oaks planted along the tennis courts might live a century
if it weren't for local vandals and imported beetles.

Through the branches of the nine big pines, the wind
sounds like oceans inside shells.

Mourning doves hoot-hoot beneath poplars. When they fly
away, their wings whinny like ponies.

Ferns in the wooded strip next to the softball diamond
smell like forests. Their fronds have freckles.

Expensive stainless steel bleachers are cold,
even in June. The wooden seats weren't safe, they say.

As if the odds were worth it, the old dog sits, waits, stares
silently up the spruce tree at the noisy squirrel.

Nearly the first day of summer. We catch sight of each other.
The only two people out walking in the rain.

The park seems empty except for us. Divided by the width
of a soccer field, we salute stiffly

as if our mere acknowledgement of each other, finally
were a beginning.

Elly Nobbs

The bird box rotted on its stand
and I was about to throw it
when fixed by a bright little eye
in a clean face of fawn down.
I tried to put the box back
but dropped it, as if bitten,
when the fledgling turned out

to have ears like dishes
on its long-tailed body
bounding under a plant stand.
The fallen box disgorged
a second jumping mouse.
In the greenhouse, in an urn,
I'd not made that pile of soil.

Uprooting the old tomato plant,
another of these mice hopped out,
eyeing me without undue alarm
and making for a corner exit
to be followed by his partner.
They'd had warm winter lodgings
for free, and spring was here.

Under the car hood in a corner,
lined with rubber, sycamore wings
were stored with seeds gnawed out.
But for these little gatherers
the front lawn would bristle with spear
and shield armies of saplings
massing to overthrow our dwelling.

Richard Lung

We all know winter shows no mercy.
It strips us and the landscape to the bone
fog and snow alternate grey blankets with white
and every living thing carries chips of ice
in its heart. The sky rests on distant hills
and we fancy we see angels or hear music.

In the still clear air sounds carry, music
travels miles. Lilting harmonies of mercy
and joy swell and tumble over the hills.
We feel faint notes resonate in our bones.
It's almost enough to drive out the ice
make us warm and glowing, alive in the white.

In the grinding cold our fingers are pinched white.
Icicles form like teeth and splinter like music.
The pond freezes solid. Ducks slip on the ice
peck at the surface hopeful for small mercies
a few crumbs to keep flesh on bones
before the sun drops behind the hills

ending another short day. We watch the hills
glowing in their sheets of snow, bright white
bathed in the light from a full moon skull bone
dome, empty shadowed sockets lacking music
unaware of emotion, but comfort and mercy
hide in the reflected rays glinting off the ice

making it brilliant, diamond-like. When ice
is beautiful and the looming enclosing hills
are softened like eyes filled with mercy
we can still be hopeful that the acres of white
will again shimmer with a different music
reaching deep, touching every bone.

We feel the coming thaw tingling in our bones.
Steady drip becomes trickle as even the thickest ice
begins to loose itself, shifting shape. A new music
a few unsteady notes from the greening hills
then swelling and rising from the receding white.
Our blood sings and we have received mercy

and winter that bares our bones and blankets the hills
winter that fills us with ice and turns our green world white
winter that plays its own music will make way for spring and
    hope and mercy.

Sindonia Tyrell

SPRING FAMILIAR

Havering winter held before it marked you
white and bent. Now you bulb damp warmth
wooding roots in me.

I poured myself
a drink for shaking out the rain to,
the alcohol sere and ripe
with aftermath, shortening days –
and you flowered from my skull
seasonal pretender.

You rise as scatter seedlings in fresh soil.
You pledge to me in frogs and chicks.
You are electric damselfly.

The garden fleshes,
outside quickens – the door –
I open you the door.

Mark Leech

The click of broom seeds flicked from
black pods in the afternoon heat
takes me to the summer of '76

where I find myself
Ambre Solaire slicked in skimpy bikini
hiding by the garden shed

sun bathing interrupted
by the whistle of the window cleaner
who will stay for gossip – with his

hare-lipped Scottish lilt
and lazy eye – if he sees me.
So I'm standing in the shadows

time marked by the intermittent rattle
and *Sweet Molly Malone*.

I wanted the sun then.
Now I sit in the shade
listening to the splitting seed pods.

    Sarah J Bryson

The sun
eats our rivers
the huts fall into disrepair
no wood, no roots
no water...

A week ago
we ate the last kapente
today the mealie loaf
but nothing
to wash it down.

All that's left
is the music
in our drum-tight skin
and even this
the maggots dance on
while we sleep.

Derrick Porter

It starts with the usual line of ripples, small crests. Some kind of meeting of the same but different, sixty degrees of separation.

The tide is coming in. The wind picks up. Rough and smooth battle over the high ground, white foam twisting and roiling all along the edge like the tail of a Chinese dragon, mobile as paper.

The sign warns of it. And now, after all this, the pebbled peninsula we stood on moments ago disappears. Horns locked, the sea closes in.

In truth it was never dependable. So the first thing to do is stop crying. Chances are you'll learn to walk along it when you can, and leave before you drown.

Patricia Debney

HAIKUS

to survive this, write…
on paper, board, screen, wall, skin –
cathartic mantras

***

remember
heat, love, butterflies
will return

***

hope thawing
this isolation –
a snowdrop

***

live the lilac hour
before the dense certainty
of black… the last breaths

Natalie Savage

There is a continent where a thousand tongues live

in Hausa, Igbo, Yoruba, the whistle and the click.
A place on earth since earth began; encircled by
The Med, The Red, Suez, and Oceans: Indian, Atlantic.

There is a land of islands of Alba's name:
Mesolithic: Rum, Eigg, Ailsa Craig;
a place of pipes and drum, where water sprites roam.

I want to plough these naked lands, the peaty loam,
the melon ground where Jumbie meets Kelpie in the
    music of time.

First, let us bless the blood of mothers wearing chains,
    who died making bread,
cleaning decks, clearing Clearings and laying down the wine.

And there is no end to it all.

My body, a lament woven into a Celtic shawl;
Hers is a harmony of sun and sour-sop; a head-tie of gold.

Mine the bone-made beads.
Hers is to walk the market road.
Mine the blood-diamond ring.
Hers is to walk the Freedom Road.

And there is no end to it all.

The stave is empty now; our body-music,
a requiem for broken dreams, an elegy
for the landscape, like some old wish is tossed
into a corner where it sits and scowls at its dreamer.

Think only of this.

Wishes lost are wasted time.

   Jean Rees-Lyons

Diary entry for 25 January 2011

The net, so fine, so white, fans out
between the reeds, over shallows so clear,
when he was a boy – not now – that he
and his father could see the fish they would catch.

But still, he leans from his boat, full of joy,
as he throws the net, though a flush of snow-melt
no longer washes the silt, the salt,
from his marshes – but still, that wind in the reeds!

From seeds they grew, lived on like memories
in land that was drained to desert, and now
they've risen, and birds come back in their thousands
as if coming back from another world.

For ever is not the point. Never can be.
It's all for now. To have been again.
The water, the nature, the fish and the birds.
It was the best feeling I have ever had.

Anne Cluysenaar

This poem was inspired by a television documentary shown on
25 January 2011 which featured the return of a Marsh Arab to
his birthplace, now recognised by scholars as the probable location of
Biblical Eden. His words are recorded verbatim at the end of the poem.

The child in the field is splitting stalks with her thumbnail
and threading flowers through the slits she's made

like the girl five hundred years before her, singing
dayseye, dayseye as she loops the string around her neck

in exactly the same way as the girl, a thousand years earlier
who's running home through a white-speckled field

letting the name her mother taught her,
dæges eage, dæges eage, thrum in her head.

*

The bees go right inside these speckled flowers
and so do her fingers, fitting perfectly into the tips

just like the paws of the redbrown fox, creeping out
at night, wearing his purple *foxes glofa*.

*

Here in the cow pasture, she finds the yellow flowers
that grow by the slops, *cusloppe, cusloppe*

and clutches a bunch of them, round as the sun.
and the girl a few centuries after her

goes cowslipping, makes balls for playthings,
strips petals for wine – *cowslips* so commonplace,

part of her parlance, she never dreams of a time
when a child won't know their name.

Elizabeth Burns

Wild splashing – a lizard
fallen in the rainwater bucket
was scrabbling at the smooth sides

frantic to be out,
delicate fingers not up to it,
flanks fighting for breath.

It's a privilege to save a life;
some people never do.
And since life is life, indifferent

to worth or benefit, it was as though
I'd saved Mahatma Gandhi, Shelley,
Barthes – or any joker

whom attentiveness and a well-placed hand
could have turned from premature extinction.
As it was, it was a lizard with no tail

I tipped, ungrateful beast,
urgent for ants, twitching for a quarrel,
into the rest of its singular career.

Carole Satyamurti

Half-eaten fries, the remains of hash browns,
fill the table's distance between them.
She scoops the car-keys, says she'll not be long.

In the washroom mirror she checks her face
close up; sees years of wearied waiting.
She steps into a sticky afternoon.

How long before he'll notice, before he'll ask –
the forecourt is nauseous with diesel and ocean –
ask if anyone's seen a woman in middle years.

She's onto the freeway, jittering across lanes.
And why, he'll wonder, now that the kids are gone,
now that they're free to hit the road each spring.

She overtakes on automatic, clearing Carolina –
recalls the one dream he has left, of building a boat;
upriver in summer; dry dock in winter. The two of them.

An unforeseen calm settles with sundown: she longs
for nightfall on unbroken stretches of highway.
It's clear ahead as far as her eyes can see.

Anne-Marie Fyfe

after seeing the painting 'Miss La La' by Degas

I remember
hanging by the skin of my teeth,
so I salute women with gritted teeth
who hang on till the time
when it's more cruel to stay than to go.

Remember me,
And don't leave it too long before you take off.
You don't even know you can fly,
but when you open your mouth,
you will remember me, and let go.

Felicity Brookesmith

REMEMBRANCE OF AN OPEN WOUND

after Frida Kahlo

Whenever we make love, you say
it's like fucking a crash –
I bring the bus with me into the bedroom.
There's a lull, like before the fire brigade
arrives, flames licking the soles
of our feet. Neither of us knows
when the petrol tank will explode.
You say I've decorated my house
to recreate the accident –
my skeleton wired with fireworks,
my menagerie flinging air about.
You look at me in my gold underwear –
a crone of sixteen, who lost
her virginity to a lightning bolt.
It's time to pull the handrail out.
I didn't expect love to feel like this –
you holding me down with your knee,
wrenching the steel rod from my charred body
quickly, kindly, setting me free.

Pascale Petit

First of all though, I should have told you
that this night is like all the others
until the very last moment.

For the past couple of days I've expected him.
Now in the kitchen he pats the back of my hand
with thick fingers. This is how it always goes.

He runs that clammy hand over my tummy, first
to feel flesh, then to rub the scales
that scissor down my body in an oil-blue sheen.

Stuck to the pads of his fingers tiny flakes
blink like a thousand terrified eyes.
He puts them to his mouth and licks.

He fans out my skin, stretches cartilage
as he wrenches apart my folds and where he holds
my back bone, I feel scars beginning from new cuts.

Later I find the hook glinting on the carpet
and suck it up with the Hoover. The other end
chokes the machine. The line is twined

around his neck and his shirt lies crumpled.

Abegail Morley

Her scales tear layer from layer, and she
slithers into clothing to conceal the sheen of skin:
shimmering purples, pearl and green.

Looking for business? the human asks.
My God, you're cold,
as cold as the sea. My God, My God, he gasps,

but God can't save him now.
He has dropped his coins in the mermaid's purse:
the King's shilling in reverse.

Those that were his feet, now fins. His legs conjoin.
She leaves him at the harbour wall,
a convert to the mermaid's cause: survival.

   Maria C McCarthy

WHY DON'T YOU JUST LEAVE?

And what if you are lost between two lives
like the woman stepping out of her dress
to swim the border river,
who knows the harrowing cold of the water
the terror of dying nameless,
a migrant spirit driven forever
like snow on the wind?

Tonight as you strike out into darkness,
you are dispossessed and risen like the moon,
as naked and streaming as the woman
who makes it to the other side,
who hauls herself out like a fish,
to stand in the first light with nothing
but the skin on her back.

   Esther Morgan

My name is Mrs Alice Ebi Bafa.
I come from Nigeria.
I'm very fine, isn't it.
My next birthday I'll be… twenty-nine.
I'm business woman.
Would you like to buy some cloth?
I've all the latest styles from Lagos,
Italian shoe and handbag to match,
lace, linen and Dutch wax.
I only buy the best
and I travel first class.

Some say I have blood on my hands
'cause I like to paint my nails red
but others call me *femme fatale*.
My father had four wives
so I've had five husbands.
I cast a spell with my gap-toothed smile
and my bottom power.
Three were good and two were bad.

The first three were old and rich
and I was young and fit.
They died of exhaustion.
The fourth one was ladies' man.
I could not count his women on one hand
but he'd rage if I looked at another man.
I was very wild when I was young.
They called me Miss Highlife,
I was not considered a good wife
but I always respected my husband.
He died when I returned from this London.

The fifth one I married for love.
He was studying law at University of Ibadon.
He was not yet twenty-one,
wicked in bed and so handsome
but he liked pornographic magazine.
His favourite was *Playboy*.
One day I threw it on fire
to teach him a lesson.
He turned into wife batterer.
He was to regret his action.
I beat him till be begged for his ancestors.
Now we get on like house on fire.

Some say I'm a witchcraft
'cause I did not bear them children.
They do not understand your Western medicine.

You like my headtie.
It's the latest fashion.
They sell like hot cake on Victoria Island.
Fifty pounds.
I give you discount 'cause I like your smile.
The quality is very good.
If I take off more I will not make profit
and I travel to Lagos next week.
Make it my lucky day.
Please, I beg you.

Patience Agbabi

CLEAN

She scrubs the taps with Ajax,
she bleaches the bath with Domestos,
she scours the bowl with vinegar and wire.
On her hands and knees, she rubs
the stains from the wood.

She takes the sheets
and the covers from the seats
and soaks them in a pint of Parazone.
She polishes the glass with a linen scrim
and spray gun of Windolene.

Then she takes a brush to her nails
and rubs until they bleed.
Her work is done, it's over –
now everything inside is clean,
no one would know he'd even been.

Michael Stewart

i am a dead woman walking asylum corridors,
with faltering step, with felted, flying hair,
with hollowed cheeks that offset bulging eyes,
with welts on my wrists, with creasing skin,
with seizures of speech and song, with a single story
between my sobbing, pendulous breasts.

once i was a wife: beautiful,
married to a merchant: shifty-eyed.
living the life, until he was lost in listless doubt –
of how, what i gave him was more delicious
than whatever, whatever had been given to me.
his mathematics could never explain
the magic of my fangled love – this miracle –
like materialising mangoes out of thin air,
like dishing out what was never there.

this discrepancy drove him to disappearance.
he moved away: a new job in another city.
he hitched himself to a fresh and formless wife.
of course, as all women do, i found out.

i wept in vain, i wailed, i walked on my head, i went to god.
stunned – shunned – shaken – shattered, i surrendered.
i sang in praise of dancing dervishes, i made music
for this world to devour on some dejected day.
i shed my beauty, i sacrificed my six senses.
some called me mad, some called me mother
but all of them led me here,
to this land of living-dead.

Meena Kandasamy

The fear that one day
we might stand with

a bed or table between us,
some domestic setting

where I'm wrapped in a towel
or lifting a lasagne from the oven

and you accuse me of never
getting over it and I accuse you

of never getting over it
and that this might take place

in a house of empty bedrooms
or very small flat (because we

won't need the space and even the dog
might be dead),

the fear that sadness will still cloud us
like scent and neighbours get used

to our puffy unhappiness.
It is the fear of that

that leads us to our bed,
where you kiss my empty hands

and very slowly I anticipate.

Rebecca Goss

The same day they
signed the divorce papers
a tornado hit the house.
I'll be damned, she said,
there goes our security.

Last September they had
to move the bed into
the dining room because
their folks couldn't use
the stairs anymore.

For fourteen years
they slept skin to skin.
This is the first pair
of pyjamas I have ever
owned, she told him.

He backed the U-Haul
into the garage to load
his graduation pictures
and the stag head
she never liked anyway.

Afterwards he never saw
the girls. She got a new
boyfriend and a red dress
which was the wrong
size so she took it back.

He moved in with his
mother's sister and she
moved the white painting
ladder from the front to the
back of the house.

She left the couch outside
on the porch when she took
the kids to live with her
in Steve's trailer half the time
with no air conditioning.

The guy at the store said
the weather's looking bad
again this year but she said
the insurance will cover it
now the State's got custody.

Cheryl Moskowitz

DEEP

Who was I that summer
I met you? Loose with desire
I moved like cream before it's churned to butter

and men I hardly knew
stopped me in supermarket aisles, B & Q,
to talk about nothing, standing closer than they needed to;

when a day without talking
to you splintered my mind – snapping
at people I loved, hiding upstairs with a phone, crying

at night; that night
you left and I sat in the dark, the polite
bones of your words sharpening with the sneak of light,

afraid of the days
opening like empty rooms, a maze
of your absence: a puzzle the years haven't erased.

Lynne Rees

that you would stamp
your own expiry date
on the end
of the packaging

choose the precise
                moment
our lives/memories
snap   separate forever

the noose
you slowly knot
to crack
        your neck
our necks

perhaps
you floated
out of your body long ago

watched your legs
twitch/jerk uncontrollably
        saw the pigment
of your own skin turn blue

but

I want to see
friction burns
bleeding fingers

the smell of red raw flesh
stricken like a match
just from trying

it's called surviving

for some time
is all I'm asking

I want to see you free
but we have different ideas of freedom

    Lorna Callery

'The wolf also shall dwell with the lamb...'
Isaiah Chapter 11 Verse 6

When we saw a fox walking beside a deer
across a field, elms behind them, we checked
with each other. Ten feet from the road as our car
shook the morning, maybe the sight that flicked
past our windows was dreamt, a shared mistake.
The fox and deer looked weary, moving
through grass towards the clearing, a break
in the hedge. We saw their faces, proving
nothing, except we dared to believe our eyes.
A fox and deer together, walking
where they intended, our lucky surprise.
I admit it gave me stupid hope, making
me ask how they found each other, how
they survived, where they might be now.

  Robert Hamberger

HARVEST

A faded photograph records the day
my father's arm was wrapped around
my mother's shoulder, their two hands
touching, a first child warmly entwined.
Fifty years later, together in a small room,
he is stooped in a chair, bones visible
through the thin cloth of skin, memories
vanishing like seeds fallen from a husk
and scattered by a sudden gust of wind.
He has forgotten the pull of a plough,
the seasons for tilling and planting.
Yet between them a shoot still grows,
blossoms, as she moves even closer,
offers a silver spoon to his lips.

  Anne Kenny

Translation of an original poem by the Roman poet Catullus

Poor Catullus, quit kidding yourself just quit
now know you've lost by admitting the losing.

There was a time when the sun shone all day long on you;
when you followed where the girl led you loved by us all as well

as we who never loved no one before. No not never nor
        after. Never.

There were plenty of the 'good times' to go around
and you wanted them all and she wanted them

from sun up to sun down it was as good as it gets.
From here on in she's not up for it and nor should you be

you jerk don't scuttle after what runs away faster after.
Don't do it. It's make your mind up time and stand firm.

Ciao, my pretty. And so today Catullus stands firm
won't say a word or come looking if you're not willing.

But you'll be sorry when nobody calls, mark my words.
God damn you love what kind of life are you looking for?

Who's calling you pretty now? What kind of guy touches you up?
Who will call you 'my love' my love? Whose will you be called?

Who will you kiss? And whose lips do you get to bite at next?
But you, Catullus, you with your mind made up stand firm.

Simon Smith

Looking beyond the contrabassoon, timps, strings,
I see you suddenly in the second row, chin supported
by your thumb, index admonishing your cheek,
crook of your third finger beneath your nose
and I can almost feel your hot dry clasp.
You can't be here, of course, listening
to these shining violins sawing farewell,
you whom we keep as ash and celluloid
in high rooms, but my eyes would have you there,
shock of white hair, bushy brows, eyes pained
by this modern noise; the solo flute struggles
against the loud, white wind of the conductor's work,
the man in the second row moves his hand,
and his mouth is a stranger as the music tips
into its climax and the bass clarinet lows
beneath the brass, saying we all carry our dead
with us on a quest for new homes, the klezmer dance
in our head propelling us forward, the fiddle pulling us back.

Sue Rose

CHAGALL

Bursts of brilliant colour on canvas:
blue skies aflame, cities luminous at last light.
The Eiffel Tower on curvy legs,
goats playing violins, firebirds,
lovers looped in eternal flight.

Your early years lived in Russia,
a humble happiness destroyed by war.
The French City of Light
and its sun-drenched south,
the crucible for your imagination.

A peaceful Jewish heart played out
its beats through your poetic paintings.
You stood apart from art movements
and let your brush dance freely,
with all the colours a child dreams at night.

Kate L Fox

i.m. D.J.E.

When hailstones scatter coldest corn
  Across the unploughed brine
And freezing gales hiss through the wreck
  Of elm and ruined pine,
When hoar-frost spreads its icy net
  On stalk and frond and spine,

The brightness of your golden flowers
  Answers the winter sun.
The noonday warmth brings out your scent
  As rich and sweet as June
When grace and toughness counterpoint
  Prickliness with perfume.

And yet your pleasures give themselves
  Only to mind and eye:
Exploring hands encounter spikes,
  Noli me tangere.
Bad luck will come to anyone
  Foolish enough to try.

The melting frost that furred your thorns
  Flashes in green and rose,
Brilliant and trembling as a star
  Until the sunlight goes
Leaving a frigid glassy bead
  Which night will crystallize,

For soon the evening chill comes on
  Warning me I should go
Back to the cosy lighted house
  Which is forbidden you,
Survivor of a darkness
  Darker than I can know.

 Janet Montefiore

The past refuses to die down, be stilled:
it rises up in savage squalls and tears
away my concentration like the north
wind scattering paper notes from my hand;

it seizes my attention like a white
crack in a charcoal sky, drawing the eye,
the sudden flurry of pigeons in leaves
above my head as I walk home alone.

In quiet moments there's nowhere to hide;
at times, when even closed eyelids won't keep
the pictures from coming all through the night,
I long to be drowned in images yet

to be drawn (what is gone is never gone,
you see, will always form a part of who
we are; when all is said and done, Donne said,
we should never question for whom it tolls).

I'm trying to forget that day: they slid
your box feet first into the fire; outside,
the sky above the crematorium
marbled with dark plumes like blood from both wrists

in bathwater; I'm trying to move on,
dipping my toe into today, but the
knell of memory keeps on hauling me
back: sounds for us and for our yesterday.

Stephen Ireland

Salvation through a pane of broken glass
is tricksy, sly, ephemeral, *unkind.*
Escape will prove unlikely till the sight
of wild blue cedars eases gnarlish minds
returning us to mottled green, *a frown*
of ochre, star-shaped, wrinkling-itchy time.
The flagrant walls of number six-six-six
are pencilled in with indecisive slips
twixt cup and lip. We'll triumph as
we draw back yellow blinds, discover when

the plum with spotted suppurating scabs
a wrinkled relic, left beside a pear
of blue-green glass, stuffed wide with bubblegum
was poisonous. You look, but cannot see
if cobwebs hide the answers, if my truth
will come to you between the rotten planks
redundant in the paint of palest blue
and speckled hen-like teeth *a sting, a dance,*
a crumbling house with balustrades, a chance,
a ha-ha, distant trees, ploughed fields. No need

for me to answer Father John's request
for railway lines through graveyards, now the park
is infrared to hide the churlish priest
whose tri-corn hat is lit with tongues of flame
to turn the cherubim to piles of ash.
And so we leave the loon beside the lake
of purple bubbles, slowly turning blue
amongst El Greco skies and strings of beads
redundant lemons, leaves, a tabby cat,
a clean device and Sirius, who swims

to Isabella's shop near Hampstead Heath
to greet her dog: a wide and angled beast
whose random paws will trip him when he runs
to church, down cobbled streets and back across
the sand *where once a filigree of twigs*
behind a building, lonesome as a song,
redeemed the boy elected on a stone
across a shining nave, so long ago.
Remember all my words when seeking your
salvation through a pane of broken glass.

Catherine Edmunds

For Oliver, shoe-designer, whose right side was paralysed
and whose speech was affected by a stroke

Hoarse, something creaks and creaks again,
out of a lagoon of mist below the hill –
late in the year, a corncrake. *Wow!*
says Oliver, a particle of language
won back. He tilts his trilby, Irish-style,
leans on his stick, its head a carved shoe.

Back in his studio, the right hand numb,
the left hand takes on its talents,
pencils arabesques of stitching, positions
precisely eyelets, studs and ridgings,
the season's designs. Undamaged, this
is his passion, his living and his language.

So much seemed lost, the man himself,
unable to articulate, more fields away
than the corncrake on the other side of mist.
Now, by week and month and year, Oliver emerges,
companioned by pain but this remaining.
The hand that draws. A love of birds. An artful brain.

Derek Sellen

Slow to cede the higher ground
and leave the ridge so lately gained
I learn to descend with dignity,
make minute adjustments, perhaps
little enough to be unnoticed
as I sidle into enormous rooms or
disappear a whole afternoon, until
walking together again by the sea
old friends I made on the way up
remark how, instead of vaulting over,
now I seem to slip under fences,
emerge somehow on the far side of hills,
glide sideways through stepped stiles
my eyes preoccupied with something
small rustling below the hedgerow,
where once I'd strut to the top
and put myself closest to the sky,
they wonder what stopped me
talking myself up, why I keep silent,
grown adept at ducking argument,
why birds are happy to ignore my
near invisible form in the shadows
as they gorge seeds I must have hung,
so then I recall that childhood fad
when being tall let you bend
your knees, double back and limbo
under the bar, the challenge being
to go closer and closer to the floor,
lowered each time to quiet applause
to less and less elevated success.

Michael Curtis

What he has been threatening he does,
lolling over to sleep on my shoulder.
His face is fissured by steady weather
but sleep has carved an expression that's quizzical,
as if an old Indian self had suddenly woken
arrowing to Kohunlich through the jungle.

A carrier bag is clutched between his feet
full of plastic knick-knacks that children want,
and marshmallows and sherbet sweets.
Bedded down over the shop, the expression finds rest
as if somewhere had fallen into place.

In pillow talk I ask him how he does it,
all that commuting between polarities,
travelling from rough shack to brash town,
sucking at a sweetness while hunger gnaws.
And I try the question that always comes to sleep
...How do you survive?

He doesn't stir. The placid look outbids the cries
of *Chicolet, Chicolet*. He makes sales in his sleep;
there's soft marshmallow so pliable to circumstance,
but I try his fizzing moment of sherbet.
It tastes like acceptance.

Bruce Barnes

They amaze me. Out of nowhere they step into step,
link arms sometimes. I shake them off. What do they want?
They keep their distance then. I wonder when they'll ask
for money, sensitive stuff – address, phone. Or try to lead me
someplace I didn't intend to go. Even when they don't, I know
I ought to know there's something seriously wrong.

But then we talk, just talk, en route to station, train.
For instance Cader, who misses home, he has a sister there.
Or Eleasidni, who says he's known as 'Sidney' and shows me
'Sidney' on his phone. They ask for nothing. I give nothing.
Small talk – where we've been tonight or where we're from,
what's different there. I'm thinking con, chancer,

still ready to kick and run, still puzzled over what it is
this young man hopes to gain, but then there's 'Safe journey',
'Nice to meet you' and smiles and holding or shaking hands.
When I'm alone, I check my bag and nothing's gone. Perhaps,
old as I am, I never acquired – or lost? – whatever it is they want.
They have lovely skin. Nice eyes. The softest brown.

Anne Stewart

A hole in the ground
was not what I wanted,
or planned.
I'd dreamt of a mansion,
a house high on a hill,
the verandah gazing eastward
to the glint of sea in the sun
– not, not at all, this ditch
which has seen better days,
the squelch of soft mud
as I wriggle down for the night,
determined to dream
of a tent, under a tree
– it's a beginning, begun.

Bernard Sharratt

LOUGAROO'S SURVIVAL

Time for feasting, a desperate love for survival:
his gentle puncturing kiss, like a lover's.

He conspires with a ripe moon
to conjure the world of folklore.

Before the moon hides in dark-grey folds of clouds,
the ritual cry: *lougaroooooooooooooooooooooo*.

There is a turbulence of sinew,
a reshaping of jaw, lengthening of canines,
knees crooking back, feet become paws with talons.

His air-nuzzling savours heifers.
In pastures they topple their bulk,
surrender pale, stretched bellies.

John Lyons

'Russian bears treat graveyards as giant refrigerators'
Headline in Guardian, *26/10/10*

On first hearing you'd be forgiven for thinking
this is some well-oiled yarn spun through
countless generations sat round winter fires,
only the heat keeping their souls alive. A tale
beginning *Once long ago, last week I saw…*
perhaps featuring Baba Yaga
tricking youths and testing maidens
or maybe Snegurochka, melted by love.

This story starts with two elderly sisters,
young in their grief, they're battling through
the bitter winds and treacherous snowdrifts,
their ever-flowing tears icicles on their cheeks.
They clutch, not flowers, this arctic wasteland
providing no such blessing, but a brush
to sweep away the snowfall
from their brother's fresh-dug grave.

Almost upon that place they freeze,
startled to see a bulky stranger kneeling,
moaning, keening. Wrapped in bedraggled fur,
he's furiously scraping at the frozen earth.
Alarmed at such violent grief
the sisters hide beneath nearby trees
and realise, too late, the stranger is no man
but an ancient forest one – black bear.

If this were a tale, a homespun one,
maybe with moral purpose or woven wisdom,
black bear would have been there to release
the brother's soul to roam his beloved forest.
Instead, we find this is some wily beast,
who coming upon a giant fridge,
munches a scavenged lunch.

    Nancy Charley

It cowered in the rotting field

somehow unscathed by worm
and rime. Ditch-water, flint-stone
and hazel kindling were all to hand.

I took enamel mug and folded blade,
forgotten by foot-forward troops
and salvaged from the churned-up soil

as I jumpily uncoiled from my wily hiding
and sidled sideways, trusting blind
my cock-a-snook

would steer me to a liberated zone,

and cradled it, this onion,
confessing, achingly, what I must do,
the truth; soup.

Whittling at the outer skin, I saw
within, white marble for my artistry,
shot with a vein of green.

Knife hit flesh,
nerve agent detonated,
taking no prisoners

in a surge of tears.

Rachel Woolf

Before daybreak and we were in among rocks,
rocks and sandy earth, very dry, carrying bags and sacks

however much each man could lift, or woman or child could lift,
water, of course, and food, whatever we'd grabbed as we left,

clothes and blankets, cups and spoons, kettles and pots.
One or two carried photographs. All the old people wore hats.

We came to a place that seemed right. Someone found sticks.
Two of the men had carried fire on their backs

and kept it alive in the usual way, so at least we could cook
rice and lentils, and boil water for tea, and smoke.

Dawn came fast: a summer sun. We could see the wrecks
out on the plain: hobbled hardware. The children played jacks

with the bits and bobs, the shiny castoffs they'd found out there
while the men sat round in a ring and debated where

next, how fast, whether in darkness, what chance...
One should be sent out, was the upshot of that; sent in advance

through the next valley, to see if the map was right, to scout
for streams or falls, perhaps to catch sight

of something familiar or safe, to sniff the wind, to choose
the way. I was the one because young and because of my shoes

which had ankle-thongs and soles from Firestone radial ATX
the better to get me across the limestone stacks.

I walked a while, then turned to take a measure with my thumb
holding it up to mark a mile, when I heard this hum

in the air, low at first but quickly growing shrill
like women in grief. I could see them, one and all,

on the rocky rise where we'd stopped; they were standing up
and looking my way. The odd thing was you could watch it slip

between the valley walls, low and going a rare old clip
and I wondered: how did it know, how did it get the drop

on a group so far out? As if it had lost them at first
but not forgotten. What happened then happened fast:

in the second before I heard the strike
I saw them ignite, all fifty/sixty or so at a stroke,

each caught in place, burning stock-still and upright
single beacons at first, then merging, then lost in their own light.

   David Harsent

Gracing the gardens of the East,
cultivated by Buddhists
in their mountain monasteries,
there exists a living fossil, a tree
with Jurassic roots.

Sparsely-branched in youth,
it fills out in old age,
veins dividing to create
fan-like leaves, bi-lobed
across the apex blade.

When a killing heat spread
in the wake of the Enola Gay,
vaporising limbs, littering the city
with human skin, the bomb designed
to wipe out one hundred thousand

in a day, did not destroy
the Ginkgo Biloba tree
just over a kilometre away,
did not stop it budding
the following spring.

And when the people of Hiroshima
re-built their temple, they split
the main staircase in half
around its trunk, carved
prayers for peace in the bark.

Victoria Gatehouse

In the precincts of the Kokutai-ji Temple
the camphor tree has been uprooted

the fireball has scorched the bark
of phoenix trees, hollowed out their trunks

stumps of temple ginkgos
scar the landscape

butterfly leaves incinerated
by the blast

no life, no greenery, our city
is a sterile wasteland

then we see the water of the Ōta river
running fresh and clear

beneath scorched earth
green roots spread

like the rainbow
when black rain fell

we will lift the phoenix trees
plant them deep among the ashes

and in summer oleander blooms
will fill the acrid air

Margaret Beston

* *Japanese: exposed to radiation*

Vitez

It is about silent children
and secret birds and the way fields hide words
and what we are doing between the trapped silences
and mothers who have hidden their dreams
and the games soldiers play with maps and villages
we have never heard of until they scream and what
happens when a man stands in his orchard and the sun
sees him and hears his music again.

The orchard is about knowledge
and what we say about returning and the way
the sniper says have a good day to his family and
cycles towards terror having fed the dog and said things
to his god, the prayers in his head making hate and as he
takes aim all he sees is a man with a blue violin.

In the orchard the man slowly takes up the blue violin,
the blue of forgiveness and what the blood does not say
and what you find if you take a dream to pieces and when you
ask a man who is very rich what he wishes to say to the
poor and when the violin sings every sniper and soldier has
this opportunity to remember the milk of a mother who is so
tired and bewildered beneath stars and garlands of grass.

The river is full of bloated moons and torn toys
and films of old men who told them about why they loved
trees and nannies who sang and the whispering dogs who
leapt out of windows barking mad and chewing on glass
before the silence arrived like a shy girl dressed in rain;
the silence of the orchard, the fallen man, his blue violin.

David Grubb

It wasn't a section of a society lost to clay
alone, or turf.
It wasn't silence
as much as replacing memory
and evidence
with a metaphor of sacrifice.

My grandmother didn't talk of famine roads
and her grandparents' hunger
but raced her beads
calling out names and addresses
in a litany.

So that my mother, impatient
at the Queen of Heaven summoned
to bless T P O'Connor
said God did not need to know
my grandfather's full name.

Still she did it
as we shuffled on our knees
gave all the details, farm and district.

Jane Kirwan

Not of my own choosing
do my paps darken like muzzles.
My belly slowly swells.
I cannot see my valley now.
I crave for lassi
but they bring us rusty water
in the bottom of a can.

They come and come,
day, night, day,
unbuttoning
as the door slaps against the stucco.
They leave our thighs and faces
crusty with their stink.

And after me,
they hump across on to my mother,
covering her shrunken face
with her heavy dirndl skirt.
She is dry, dry.
Her womb is a husk.

Each day I am ripening.
I do not want this cuckoo
fluttering its rabid wings
in my darkness.
I can see its wild eyes beneath my skin.
It will suck me dry as rock.

Yet, I have practised its birth –
how I will keep my legs far apart,
my eyes screwed shut,
then roll it with my heel in the dust
kicking it and its afterbirth
down the mountainside.

Or, how I will say, *Give me my baby,*
and boy or girl, call it Katya.
That was my mother's name.

   Pat Borthwick

Grass grown high over
her place, her space.
Stomach struggling against
ground, tongue
licking soil,
she waits.

Wanted, sought, hunted,
khaki caressing
grass, salvation beyond
her grasp, she
knows. Peering through
gaps, shoulders slump,
gun lowers.

Desertion her crime,
refusal to kill lambs, objections
unheeded – not her
conscience: charred bodies
her companions. Here she
hides, any
place any time
from My Lai
to Fallujah.

Shots. Animated, she scuttles
butter soft through
earthy mud,
heart punching, crying.
She wishes time could
invert, that she were home,
in the womb.
She can't: choices have
been made, dice have been
cast. She will be pursued.
Always.

Luigi Marchini

There is nothing
like the smell of dead bodies.
It hit her as soon as she walked in,
lime, dead bodies.

Tables piled high,
heads protected by hands,
limbs blown off, some covered,
some naked.

She said the survivors
dug up the mass graves
carried the broken bodies
to the school

where 27,000 had been killed.
They'd wanted the bodies
for proof that the genocide
really happened

wanted the world to see.
She said she had to leave
couldn't stay inside any longer
but she brought back the images.

In an interview on the radio,
she tried to explain it.
I wrote her words down
to remind me.

Catherine Whittaker

The heavy swell of history
has beached us here
so many stranded sailors
wild-eyed and salt-spattered
huddled before a congealed horizon

I close my eyes
and count the years
between these painted battles
the seconds between ambulances

Kiefer's cursive script
has decoded Chlebnikov
and given us all
a number to play with
like a toy submarine in the bath

And this choice of corrugated steel
has proved propitious
blitz-like and eerily appropriate
as we share phones with strangers
like spam or bovril

Outside in Hoxton Square
sirens again

Inside equations chase their tails
trying to make sense of war

    Gillian Laker

Here, to this city garden,
soldiers come from battlefields
of rock and sand. Within high walls,
they trundle barrows,
water, dig and hoe,
coil twine round saplings.
With roughened hands, they scoop up
moist brown earth, inhale its fragrance,
let it trickle through their fingers
as rain falls on faces at ease now.

And see, over there they are planting
poppy seeds to honour those
who served with them
but weren't so lucky,
didn't make it back,
whose faces they remember
beneath hostile skies,
a harsh sun glinting on their weapons
and shining in their eyes.

Linda White

AN OLYMPIAN IN SOMALIA

Your night training was ten thousand knee jerks –
implosions whilst asleep, the dream-repercussions of a sport
where those in the lanes alongside are as quick,
but only with mortars.

Come that glorious day, you wake to another gun and
        go to work –
to face down The Straight of No More Weaving. The stats
in triple figures show the quick and the dead bit down to
        the quick:
your lesson in how to tell reports

of friendly fire apart.

Rupert Smith

Or, 'What I learned about boys in the military'

1. When they meet you for the first time
   They'll call you 'Ma'am'
   This is a habit they never truly get out of.

2. They are the only men alive
   who know how to polish their shoes.

3. When they're pulled over by the police
   they'll give their registration number
   in the phonetic alphabet.

4. They don't like to be called
   'our brave boys'

5. They're taught to speak from the stomach,
   like opera singers,
   but that doesn't mean their voices never get hoarse.

6. They drive their bayonets into sandbags to practise,
   but they also talk to their pillows at night.
   Rehearsing their letters home.

7. Even if you ask, they won't tell you what they've seen.

8. They deal with the months just fine,
   it's the days they can't take.

9. Their flags gather dust.

10. At night, when they think you're asleep,
    they talk to the men they killed.

Christopher R Moore

Lost three mates in Belfast
Lost two fingers at Fox Bay
Lost my nerve in Mitrovicë
Lost my wife along the way
Lost my kids, my home, my future
Lost my medals, lost my pride
Drank my pension to forget it
Lost my bearings, almost died

Hey you, get out my doorway
Bugger off, you stink of gin
Find a doss house, if they'll take you
I would never let you in
You're a drain on our resources
You're a waste of blinking space
It's a pity that you're breathing
Men like you are a disgrace

Who is this fool before me
Does he have the least idea
What it's like to see men dying
How it feels to live in fear
Has he watched a troopship burning
Smelt a human's roasting skin
Has he heard young soldiers crying
I've killed better men than him

But he doesn't need to know that
He is free to speak his mind
After all that's what I fought for
Can't complain if it's unkind
He might also have his demons
He might also have his dread
But he has no right to judge me
Less, to wish that I were dead

Bob Le Vaillant

7 July 2005

She wanted night
to turn back to morning
when she was alive and running
for the Number Thirty.

> She'd hear the girls – *late again*
> when they tittered at her messy hair,
> her strangely unsuitable clothes,
> her breathless apology.

> She'd see her lover through glass
> behind that big desk –
> no evidence of passion, except perhaps
> the tingle of half-smiling lips.

She wished night
would run itself back
so she could swear
when the doors closed

and the bus left without her.

Valerie Morton

I split logs, crumple *The Times*, read again
how Guantanamo detainees pour water,
let it soak in overnight, use plastic spoons
to scratch enough earth, press in seeds
saved from meals: pepper, cantaloupe, lemon.
It's old news. My grandfather's
seven years hard labour became ten,
when gulag guards searched the hut roof,
found three apple pips planted in cans
he'd bartered for bread. I strike a match.

Back in Kharkov, free but coughing blood,
my grandfather grafted, taught me
to heel in tiny saplings, excited
by an orchard of cherries
he'd never taste. He died digging up turnips.
I close the stove, stay crouched
by my weeping grandmother, in the yard
where the tap had burst. For days
she wouldn't speak, just carved the ice
into a frieze of sunflowers and life-size trees.

Sue Butler

A small boy is running.
The town, its tenements and courtyards,
shops and stalls close in on him, as if
the town itself were holding its breath.

He was still asleep when Aunt Wika
left for her shift at the hospital,
so he didn't know they would march in
along Ulitsa Wesnina this morning.
Every day she leaves earlier –
and returns even later.

As long as the soldiers' boots keep
time on the cobbles of Ulitsa Wesnina.
Making the sound of a thousand
cockroaches crushed.

If only he had a red handkerchief
he could tie round his arm
like everyone else. If only
his mother had sewn him an armband,
but she's gone inland, to look for his father,
to St Petersburg perhaps.

As long as the soldiers don't disperse
to walk down Ulitsa Gorkova looking for
pretzels or chocolate…

If he can just squeeze through a gap
in the wall behind the Orthodox church.
His grandparents are in bed waiting for him –
too old to get up any more.

Another hundred steps to reach
the sandy road at the edge of town.
If he can carry this loaf of bread home,
this loaf he's holding in both hands.

Maria Jastrzębska

It wasn't easy. He was still flying
missions then, navigating the Lancaster
accurately into the flak, into the foul-mouthed
shafts of the searchlights. Fifteen shaken minutes
from the aerodrome through the thin November dawn
on his motorbike and he was home. She was up
already with Tim in the scullery
putting the nappies to boil in the bucket.
Only one, the only one, he wouldn't be held,
stiffened against him, struggled and wailed.
It was tiredness, he told himself, tiredness and cold
that had set the tic going again in his eyelid.
Tilted by the child, she poured him stewed tea
and he took it to bed warming his hands
a little round the thick white china.
Later aware of a murmur in the hall
he guessed she was strapping him in, manoeuvring
the pram, and he drifted off as silence settled.
At the Co-op she collected the butter ration,
at Willis' pig's liver for their tea,
and then she came home the long way round
beside the motionless cloudy canal
where only a mallard made v's on the water.
Tim fell asleep as they reached the gate
and suddenly limp from the broken nights
she flopped down by dad in the blacked-out room.
In that half hour before Tim whimpered
I began, though I was nothing to them.
As they slid apart, one of next door's hens
started clucking and mum almost tasted new laid
eggs for lunch – she'd ask Betty – but dad couldn't take
his eyes off the barrage pounding up
as they came in low for their final drop.

Michael Laskey

A walk might shunt me up the gears.
Desperate, I fetch coat and hat, wind my scarf,
tuck in. I venture up the valley. Up through scrub
to where the scent of pine ribbons gelid air.

Whorls of needles like bottle brushes.

Ahead a man crouches
to run fingertips lightly over a trunk.
He frowns, peers, bends nearer,
passes his hand over yet again
as if half-blind.

                    Yet he has no stick,
no guiding dog. He bends so close
his head grazes, then straightens,
moves on to stroke another, then another,
exploring with a doctor's touch.

The war, he mutters. *On leave.*
A German fighter saw me, turned,
let rip a burst of fire. I hid behind a tree.
Just here. Am searching for the bullets.

It will have grown, I say. *Look higher.*
Ah. He raises his eyes. *Ah yes.*
Yes. Now I see.

He pats rough bark, caresses with his palm.
This tree, he says. *This tree. We're friends.*

   Marilyn Donovan

Cold, yes, under a sodium sky at three o'clock in the morning.
But there's this shawl to wear and tea with Manuka honey.

And across the only gap in the border, a thousand refugees
        an hour
pouring through Ras al-Jedir. An hour? By morning, my morning,

another five thousand, by lunchtime, another five and how many
have even a striped hemp blanket? Fifteen thousand blankets!

Imagine one. The way it folds stiffly as a tent around the head
bent back, the shoulders jutting, knees drawn up, wrists free,

the lone triangular edifice. Feel the weave. Hairy, ridged.
Smell it. Determine the sightlines either side of the hollowed
        cheeks.

Imagine the scene in silence, not as it would be. The blanket
as a block, a wood carving. The tools: straight gouge, spoon
        gouge,

back bent, dog leg, fishtail chisels, V-tools, punches, vices;
hook knives, drawknives, rasps and rifflers, mallets, saws,
        abrasives;

slip waterstones – how quiet they sound – and strops for
        sharpening.
Figure in a blanket. In acacia, sycamore or, most likely, olive.

   Mimi Khalvati

It is Bristly Ox-tongue,
too shy to speak.
Long silence.
It is Bristly Ox-tongue.

Who stands rooted
with his white hair uncombed.
Long silence.
He stands rooted.

He stands rooted
with his white hair uncombed,
pulling it out in handfuls.
This is no good.

Long silence.
He carries this silence everywhere,
like an implement from long ago,
he carries it everywhere.

This is Bristly Ox-tongue.
Long silence.
He has enormous jaws, chewing on silence.
He has enormous jaws, chewing on silence.

This is no good.
He has come indoors in his boots
and anyhow, his hands are more like hooves.
This is no good.

If only he was among his own kind,
rutting and feeding by night, hiding by day.
Long silence.
I said if only he was among his own kind.

If only he was among his own kind
standing in groups by the roadside
or making small clumps on the cliffs.
Now that would be good.

Alice Oswald

This world of soggy wadding ends
in a blur a hundred yards from every step.
The whole morning, mushroomy and muted,
is buried in fog.

A multitude of spiders has been at work for hours
drawing down soft bundles of it, pulling it thin,
                              spinning it thinner,
                                   thinner,
                    swinging on it,
                running with it trailing from pillar
to post: a precise drill perfected
with little evolutionary flourish
over tens of millions of years.

After all that energetic angular care
those fog-structures,
        those larder-castles in the air
are sagging, tearing,
        bearing
no wriggling protein flies
but strings and strands of juicy silver drops
and the odd scrap of gold leaf caught
                              mid-fall.

In an almost-human land
figures happen: spectral suits of armour,
protean knights conjured from the edge,
and there's the sweep and rush of sudden dragons,
eyes searching in quadruplicate.

Back in the empty house, your hair a clammy nest,
you think you understand the hidden birds you heard
damped down, depressed by that moist weight of sky
to a subdued *chink*.

            And how the spider might feel
    swaying
            in the ruins of her foggy web.

Jo Field

When I see the tallest tree has been felled
and count the rings in the stump
I remember the way the frost
decorated it each winter with stars.

Mary Robinson

SURVIVAL

At the summer solstice, the sun
in Cancer breeds vulnerable,
tenacious, excitable
crustaceans programmed to triumph
against odds; in water, on land,
balancing their destiny
with grace, not unlike women
carrying water, stones, children,
on their heads, shoulders, arms –
the body transformed into
a miracle, a vessel for survival.

Crabs, lobsters, beetles, scarabs,
snails, turtles, tortoises –
all self-contained, sensitive creatures –
supporting their crosses on their backs
negotiating in an uncertain,
unpredictable, unforgiving world;
making themselves at home everywhere,
being eternally prepared.

Alert to their surroundings,
shielding themselves from danger,
they adorn their armour –
faith that arrives like leaves in spring.
For these guiltless warriors,
only one out of a hundred
of thousands will survive their spawning.

Shanta Acharya

When he was born they had to cut out his heart: it had rotted in
the womb like bad fruit.
He's a loner it's true, but you'd barely know he's different, except
the way his T-shirt pulses
around the dip in his chest, and how he stares at our fighting and
falling in love.

Sometimes you see him on the street watching a couple embrace
or a lost child crying.
He puts a hand on the hole, like a man who has lost a leg thinks
he can walk.
You'd think he'd always cover it up, but sometimes he stands out
in a field, eyes closed

shirt off, letting the breeze blow right through. His veins around
the wound ballooning
like a frog might breathe, testing the strength of his skin against
the force of air.
He knows we're looking, enjoys our curiosity, our envy. It's like
he's singing

this is who I am, a man with no heart as he gazes at the patchwork sky,
head aloft.
We wonder how our rag and bone hearts keep going, and each
time we lose someone,
it helps to think of him, the cool breeze in the field.

   Cath Drake

Unwanted as an elderly employee who's slowed down,
the car's been bumped over the brook in the park, stripped
of identity on the gravel under the viaduct

and abandoned by an owner who couldn't care less
that he's torn willow leaves, calm,
in his itch to turn the key in a faster model.

Every day I see how irresistible helplessness is,
wince at the wrenched wheel lying
like a lost foot. Nearby, spattered with dust,

the lopsided body peers through a ragged hole
and from the ground a hail of glass protests sharply.
Soon the felt carpet is rucked and fuzzed

as if by a factory of mice. I wonder if a fisted hand
walloped the back of the plastic baby chair
until it broke, if it was satisfying to knife the upholstery,

chuck condoms from the passenger window.
One sultry day I find the car burnt to death, its sides
unfleshed, the seats skeletal juts, the last shreds

of dignity snatched from the steering wheel,
the crown of the head rubbed gold
with rust. The air is still acrid with the smut of words

and I can smell the hot desire to destroy,
see how it ballooned as orange tongues licked
with fervour until fire gripped the mute frame. The murder

roaring in my ears threatens to swallow the energy
that cooks a meal, offers kindness, plans a bridge,
begins processes in the quiet of a womb, egg, cocoon,

which culminate in the black butterfly I've just seen
in the copse with red squares across its wings,
the rook on this tar-stained path, its beak tugging

at a paper bag full of bread, myself unravelling thoughts,
and the must insistent as the heart's pump, as breath
that pushes us through pain, through loss.

Myra Schneider

I collect odd shoes, pay pennies
at jumble sales, gather them
from roadsides, the high-tide line.
Old boots, sandals, trainers, lace-ups,
pumps, stilettos. All single.
I lay them side by side by size,
baby's knitted bootie to workman's boot,
see them scuffed and empty.
I reread the recipe, reclassify

by material, fraying fabric, split plastic,
shrivelled leather seasoned with sea salt.
I dissect the animal skin, discard cloth
and metal, broken heels and laces,
pour a gallon of water, stir sugar
and yeast, drop one shoe
after another into the bucket.
The fermenting leather retraces itself.
Escaping bubbles carry away the bitterness

of uphill paths, roads not taken,
lost races, missed goals, unnoticed
first steps and abandoned last dances.
I sip the wine, swallowing summer
holiday sweetness, hopscotch,
skipping, paddling, wading
through waist-high wheat.
I siphon forgotten footsteps
into green glass, saving them
for when I need to just sit.

   Nicky Gould

Genie-like he appears when needed,
this man with no watch, no literacy, no home.
A clap of the hands and he's gone.

In Bombay bazaars he's bartered for his mistress
before the maid has brought her morning tea.
She inspects both sides of his hands before

he peels, pounds, prepares the masala
that makes pungent the day's meals,
his tools: knife, stone slab, rolling pin.

Her face hardens in the scolding of him:
the core of their relationship. Head bent,
he plays dumb – he knows his part by rote.

For this volubly silent subjugation
he thanks his gods each day,
his village a 20-mile walk away.

Barbara Dordi

She finds it difficult to smile
in a way that is not upsetting.

One side of her upper lip
refuses to co-operate. The other

over-compensates, exposes
too much of her teeth, and she looks

like a dog losing its patience.
Her left eye is half-shut

and the right stares straight ahead,
permanently surprised at the world.

Her hair – scraped across skin – skirts
an ear reduced to little more

than a hole. Who knows how well
she can hear? But she speaks,

coherently and without tears,
about the day, five years ago,

just turned 20, when a man, sent
by another man, greeted her

with hydrochloric acid.
What remains undisclosed

is where either of those men
are now, whether even

they are able to show their face,
or if after that time, in any other

meaningful way, they left their mark.

John Mackay

I am tied to this world by hope. It is all I have.
Though life has played its best tricks on me;
it grabbed my grandiose world-beating dreams
by the heels and cast them head-first
into bottomless pit latrines full of maggots.
They were dreams so sweet I wrapped myself
in blanket and dreamed them three nights straight.
Yet I smile like the wise old fool I am,
believing tomorrow's dreams will be bigger.
I crave living, drumming the drum of life.

I am tied to this world by hope. What else is there?
Supine upon my burning bed of sorrow
I collect my falling tears in a shallow basket,
it is woven with ten interlocking fingers
cupped just above my naked navel.
I know these tears are raining,
but why can't I see them, or feel them. Why?
There is a montage of scenes in my head,
I am doing time in a cinema of surreality. Yet,
I stand living, drumming the drum of life.

I am tied to this world by hope. It is my fate.
I am accustomed to grey moments, laughter
dances in lifesquare, black-eyed like a woman
who chooses to love and to hold, though knuckled
about by her drunken lover. I forgive friends
who dissect my demons in the worlds
of Blackberry Messenger and Whatsapp.
The devil comes to sit on my shoulder, he whispers,
Drive off the edge of Woodford Bridge at 90mph,
That's a great place to claim your lights out.
He fails to get my signature on the contract, this time,
I choose living, drumming the drum of life.

So I play a little trick of my own; I live.
I suspect that someday every good thing will be mine,
though manacled by countless ropes of pain and despair
I have to show life who is boss; me! I am the boss,
that's why I'm still living, drumming the drum of life,
tied to this world by hope. Hope, my victory song.

Nnorom Azuonye

Delia's scarlet varnish is chipped
like most of his nails. He asks for milk,
three sugars and puts 10p in the tin
for extra biscuits.

Florrie won't talk to him, shifts table
when he moves close. Lousy bitch, going off
with Reg last night. It's no joke, alone
on the station floor.

Delia's lost his broken brolly. In from the rain
his make-up dribbles down wet cheeks
peacock, tan and black, spattering stubble
round a molten mouth.

Every Wednesday, Seamus comments on
Delia's shapely legs and ankles, snagged
Jacob's ladders leading heavenwards
up his wool mini-skirt.

When Delia's in the mood, you're in stitches;
he belts out smutty stories in that butch voice,
tells you what happened on the tram, in church,
at the Oxfam shop.

When Delia's feeling peevish, he spits
venom, blames the Pope, lashes out
and gets thrown off the premises
without his dinner.

It's quiet without Delia, no laughs. He sulks
like this sometimes. Then he's back
with a new coat, new shoes, new yarns,
nicotine smile.

It's dismal without Delia. They found him
in the canal, his tights round his neck
face a mess. Now Florrie can sit
wherever she likes.

Mary Scheurer

Philosophical, polite,
accepting
beyond her years,

grateful even
for coffee
and two plain biscuits.

Beneath bottle-brush hair
she wore her black eye
like a badge,

her battle fatigues
a man's top coat
with turned-back cuffs.

Seventeen, she said
she was, but
she didn't look it,

no permanent address
to satisfy the DSS, just
70p in her pocket.

No complaints
about being dumped back
outside like garbage.

I know how it is, she said.
*You've got your rules
to keep to.*

A visit to the loo,
quick wash, shoes re-stuffed
with paper towels

and she was gone
into night streets, the rain
sharpened by an icy wind.

With practised cynicism
she'd shrugged off Christmas lights
beading the city square

and canned choirs
filling the shivering skies
with Glorias.

Moira Andrew

GOING MISSING

she doesn't want any part of her body
to go missing

when she cuts her fingernails
she saves each new horn of a second moon

in a waterproof box
where they lie

like scales
of transparent fish

she hasn't cut her mermaid hair
since she was 12 years old

if she ever does she says
it will join the fingernails

weaving calypso rhythms
into filaments of silk

Caroline Carver

I woke up this morning
  And I didn't feel blue
Yeah, the day was dawning
  And I felt brand new –
I didn't have the blues
  They'd gone just like the dew:
Tell everyone the news
  O, I'm not sad and blue.

O, I'm not sad and blue
  Mama, and I don't why
O, I'm not sad and blue
  O, I'm a different guy,
Could be this sunny day's
  The one I've waited for
The blues have gone away,
  They've walked out the door.

I went to the river,
  My blues all washed away,
I looked in the water
  And saw the sunlight play.
O, how could I be blue
  When I felt so fine
O, how could I be blue
  With a life like mine?

  John O'Donoghue

ALWAYS THE LAST MORNING

there would be low sun hugging the rocks;
the sea knew, and deepened its blue like a bruise.

Leaving the house and the low-voiced packing,
the dust-sheeting of chairs and beds like corpses,
she fled one last slow marvelling time
over slant-lit common and worn-out dunes
to the empty strand, where salt-silence whistled;

plucked the moment whole; zipped it into her jerkin;
a cold plum for comfort back home.

  G B Clarkson

I lived in a white prison
white beds, white uniforms
colourless covers, bandages
a ceaseless cheery sound bleaching us out.

I was taken outside by a nurse. She had
warm skin, dark eyes, and beauty spots
she wore a pleated cap, a scarlet cloak
we talked. She pushed me

to the shoe shop in my dressing gown
over pavements, up and down steps.
I saw ordinary people
not lying down. Not hurting.

My cotton-wool feet, after six months
unconstrained, nude, forgotten
surprised me. Two sizes bigger
though they had not touched the ground.

She took me in a wheelchair to buy slippers
to learn to walk again
yellow flowers on dark red velvet
straps round the ankle
a bead button.

Harriet Proudfoot

At first a horror-film thrill at the razor wire that
garlanded the hospital. Sat in the waiting room
holding her breath beside the other outpatients
who were unexploded bombs liable to go off
BANG. Scrabbled in her bag for a book as
defence against the man in rumpled clothes who
tossed random phrases at her like a lonely kid
trying to entice someone to play ball with him.
Looked up eagerly each time a consultant or
therapist greeted their clients with the impeccable
manners of maitre Ds overlooking the foibles
of the very wealthy. But after several appointments,
she and her therapist would remark upon the
weather whilst navigating the hospital's computer
game of locked doors and forbidden levels.
In the coffee bar watched with animal indifference
as the inpatient assistant slowly calculated her
change as if it was foreign currency. Ate her
sandwiches in the grounds, watching squirrels
caper, occasional screams issuing from acute
wards indigenous as the cry of seagulls by the coast.

Fiona Sinclair

THE DNA LOTTERY

The unseen knife steals
Slivers of cells from deep within
And slathers on slides
This bodily bullion
Like pip-packed strawberry jam
For goggle-ensconced eyes
That morph men into bugs
Whose latex-encased fingers
Borrowed from shop-window mannequins
Dissect and discover and discard
So when the drugs wear off
The detached doctor delivers the verdict:
Your days aren't as numbered as once was feared.

Anne-Marie Jordan

Standing among the waiting passengers at Victoria
I know what you are waiting to hear.
Through the yawning gap the train arrives;
finding a car and counting the minutes
I catch a glimpse of the black mass
enfolding the steel spikes beside the tracks
Hedera helix
and say nothing.

All day I have been tossed and crushed –
so many people intent on something or somewhere
else. Outside the window, bits of broken brick
and drink boxes litter a scarred earth, a few
thin stalks fight their way through the tarmac;
I retreat to my forest of words: *remission, metastasis.*

Then slowly arching forward and away
we cross the river at Battersea, lurching through
industrial wasteland where heaps of rubbish displace
the river's grey froth; on the other bank
a mannequin's torso, armless, legless
with breasts exposed, gazes into her future.

We pass her too and further,
fields of flattened cars melt away
into leafy suburbs of swimming pools
and trampolines, left by summer and children.
I'm without words to say how much I need you
as the train clicks eastwards, the trees-of-heaven
retreat, and I pretend that life starts
here where the sun breaks through.

    Nancy Gaffield

Tangled hair, charcoal-socket eyes,
mouth slack after one more long night
restless on my back. This body's fenscape,
manscaped, hills removed – the meaty joins
still livid, tight shut mouths
where distant territories were stitched

in touch. Blood seeps in deltas over ribs,
yellow and purple track to the waist.
You're even more beautiful now, you say
and I believe, for though I never was, I am
explorer, seeker – I've travelled
and I have an ear for truth.

  Clare Best

SURVIVING

You should get your hair cut, mother,
it doesn't suit your face like that.

They're right, I know,

but I have seen my skull
riding on my neck

bold and bald as a moon.

When the first faint fleece grew back
I threw away the hats

and let it grow.

Daughters, I do not need it cut
to know how hair can fall.

  Gill McEvoy

I did not live in houses.
I flew home to them in quick spurts
of remembrance.
On the wings of wishes.
With parents' faces overlapped upon a house
glimpsed briefly and an address
kept on a scrap of paper in a wash-bag.
I lived on the end of syringes.
In the ruby drop that trembled
before the needle was discarded.
I lived wrapped around the silver-tips
of thermometers and in other people's hands.
I lived between the harsh light of morning
and the dimmed lights of the nightshift.
I lived between the last gasp of a child's
breath and cold white sheets left behind them.
I lived between a pillow's crackling starch
and a cold stethoscope.
Limbo was my place.
Held in that sharp sliver between life and death –
hygiene and bacteria.
All touch clinical as though emotion
would bring contamination and a smile
contain contagion in its open mouth.
I sighed through each day and hoped in vain
that I would hear the words
Better now. You won't have to come back.

Miki Byrne

i.m. Nathan Kelley 22.04.61–14.12.85

This Christmas he's been dead
longer than he was alive.
He had twenty-four years
of learning about fish

and what makes them tick.
Of winters floating in warm seas
where fish were as if
a child had painted them.

In photos he's grinning,
not showing the shark-bite
scars of heroic surgery,
nor the years gasping for breath

drowning in air.
Not showing the weeks treading
water in wards of old men
whose hearts also failed

and where he could not bear
to waste precious time,
but instead read books on fish disease
and the geology of planets.

He shelters now in the shallows of my heart,
and on the oddest of occasions,
for example, when I see a tank of guppies
in a waiting room, a jar of winter daffodils,

or a full moon blueing the bay,
he rises to the surface,
and like his fond goldfish,
Carassius auratus,

the flaming stargazers, whose
celestial eyes followed his every move,
he's still there in the current of life,
with me wherever I go.

Ann Kelley

Blackout:
I'm flying face-downwards through
a cylindrical tunnel; electrical storms
explode, lightning-flashes glance off metal
surfaces, startled fireballs roll, erupt,
the metallic clang of closing doors
bombards my eardrums;
gale-force winds blast my cheeks,
whip my hair to rats' tails,
flatten my hands against my thighs
as I torpedo westwards –
portholes thunder shut, leaving me
with snapshots, flashcard impressions
of past lives, vacant worlds,
a nineteen forties living-room,
an empty nursery, a cluttered kitchen,
computer stations – scanners, printers – onwards,
gathering speed past a deserted playground,
a country church, a wooded hillside
thick with snow, towards
                    a chrysanthemum of yellow light.

Twenty, nineteen, eighteen, seventeen,
she's coming back – sixteen, fifteen,
she's almost there, fourteen, thirteen –
my heart drums against my rib-cage –
twelve, eleven – the helicopter whirr
of a bee's wings and its body bouncing
off the window, mad bent on escape – *ten, nine,*
come on, you can do it… I open my eyes...
note tubes, drips, the doctors bending over me;
a nurse is rubbing my hands, another
supports me as I turn my face to greet
the sun's warmth, crying
                    for the living hell of it.

June English

X-rays pinned to a glowing wall, the smell...

I can't quite see. On my face, something
plastic, a woman gently moves my hand
to another place beneath my sight
and in which, oddly, I cannot quite believe.
It's cold.

The fingers aren't reporting promptly either –
I shall write them up in my little black book,
using the minute pencil which came attached.

Oh, here's a man. The smell of...
well there's plastic, of course, but something else.

Is he talking to me? Is he talking to her?
A jolly sort with a bushy moustache
he's trying to conceal with a paper mask
that looks a bit concerned.

Did the lights just flicker then?
The wall's a different colour
and who's this younger foreign guy
talking to his watch?

Wait... did I miss something?

Ian Badcoe

On a day black as the insides
of chests before the *katchinas*
locked up sun and moon, locked the world
in darkness, a man who's suffered
a stroke is being kept alive
by exquisite means. Of great weight
admittedly. But what of those
nameless slight brought down for reasons
not natural, we try our best
to keep *them* out of plywood chests?

You'd think it was the sun itself
there on the ventilator, *its*
satellites in terror their world
will once more be locked in darkness.
How we choose for whose life we fight.

Too late for ones herded in chests
on wheels, ridden by *katchinas*
drunk on might, heading towards chests
with flues; or the moon-faced poets
contained by exquisite means in
regimes *not* to be brought down
by weight of outspoken reason –
friends grieved in secret, so much so
you'd think they weren't grieving at all –
so much so, was hard to tell they'd
any feelings. Poets and friends
who only blinked to be accused
of anything, by aides anxious
themselves to survive the antics
of *katchinas* – wresting back sun
coyote had released, scaring
even brave moon into hiding.

They say today the stroke victim
opened one eye, and even blinked
as though the chest's lid had lifted
a chink, forestalling a future
without his radiant power –
it was denied in the hour.

Deborah Trayhurn

Katchinas: evil spirits of American Indian legend

I glimpse a strange truck
in the nearside lane
with a soiled ribbed hose
wound on a two-metre reel
like a toy fire-engine
and up close to the cab
balanced and symmetrical
a pair of translucent
sepia-coloured tanks
I can't imagine what for
swirling with what seems
nothing more than water
as the truck moves and crawls
on the Great Cambridge Road
the sun so high its rays
split and crack and sashay
in the tanks to the truck's
stop and start the little dance
between brake and pedal
every vehicle performs
and as I draw alongside
the liquid's filled with the frisk
of the light so fluently
refracting full of bows
and slabs and S-shapes
glinting like lemon bars
anaemic and ruinous
and rather than the road
I see a man who was dying
who lost his sight slowly
who I sat with sometimes
maybe twenty years ago
and back then I'd imagine
how I might be his eyes
having words to convey
what he would never see
though my mouth stayed
shut I kept my eyes open

Martyn Crucefix

If her spine were not
fusing slowly to itself,
each knuckle raw
as bruised plums,

succulent with pain –
encrusted salt
that lays like coral,
microns at a time,

within the joint –
some grit beneath
an eyelid, the broken
stone of peach,

an anger salved, applies
the patience of a clergyman
with villagers who grieve.
She fingers them,

manipulates complaints
removes their old tools,
undoes the workman's
belt, to place herself

upon the battered
bench. Along which, if
she did not stretch
each morning, slender,

keep her weight low
beyond a miracle
she would break
when in my grip.

I've seen her swim,
so quick with silence
steal within the moments
when we should speak,

introduce oneself, make
light with humble words.
My tongue has slowed.
It cannot curve or bend.

Richard Moorhead

When after a mutiny of waiting your name was called
and you swarmed with a thousand others onto the ship
that would take you home, you found
you suddenly couldn't bear the intimacy
of men, the heat that was not the heat of the open
but heavy with trapped sweat and voices crying
to unknown people, the confusion
of those who had forgotten how to sleep deeply.
You joined the stampede upward as dusk fell,
bagging a space for your hammock if you were swift enough
or lucky, or stretching out under the stars
you knew so well by now, their company
shifting imperceptibly as you crawled out of the tropics.
Dozing too long, you were caught out by the crew
who hosed the deck at dawn, a soaking
without warning; becoming ill and more ill
up the west coast of Africa, mistreated for malaria
while your fever blossomed – you no longer knew
where you were or had been, were colourless
beneath your skin. By Southampton
it was touch and go, you were ambulanced to Emergency
where they drained the fluid like seawater
from your lungs and you were left to slowly
recover yourself: no celebrations for you, no partying
in the streets – but you were alive, you lived:
take your time, they murmured
as you began the journey back, just now and then
having these dreams still, seeing Lily with her basket of jackfruit
rolling among the men, or a snake roof-slithering
after a rat; or rocking frozen in the cradle of a high wind
watching bags of flour burst hundreds of feet below,
metal clamped to your skull, voices saying things
you knew must be important if you could only
remember the code, if they would speak
a little louder, allow your head to clear
as it would, it had to, it couldn't stay like this forever.

Caroline Price

I've pruned the roses, cut back herbaceous
shoots and stems and planted primulas in pots,
so you can see a little colour from the window
when you get home. Now I'm on my knees
with knife in hand, weeding pavers.

Dandelion, couch grass and yellow-flowered
oxalis, till my fingers find a tiny, hairy seedling
that my eyes identify as comfrey, *knit-bone*,
and I smile, because it seems a good omen,
as if this life is still willing to give you
what you need.

Miles away in that hospital bed you are
a flightless, featherless, gawky baby bird;
secondary growth excised, two new titanium
branch lines shoring up your spine.

You said once your name means snow in Spanish.
Well it can only be the kind of snow that falls
way above the tree line, high up on the *sierras*.

Powdery and dazzling.
Snow at its best.
Snow that persists.

  Anna Dickie

Imagine thirst without knowing water.
And you ask me what freedom means.
Imagine love without love.

Some things are unthinkable,
until one day the unthinkable is here.
Imagine thirst without knowing water.

Some things we assume just are as they are,
no action is taken to make or sustain them.
Imagine love without love.

It is fear that eats the heart: fear and
endless talk, and not risking a step.
Imagine thirst without knowing water.

Fold away your beautiful thoughts.
Talk away curiosity, chatter away truth.
Imagine love without love.

Imagine believing in the whispers,
the screams and the gossip. Dancing to a tune
with no song to sing inside you.
Imagine love without love.

John Siddique

It's awkward on the butcher's slab
with artery and clavicle peeping
from the red sweat of the accident.

It is necessary to speak of the silver
and the gleam and the very hard lights
which hang and sway in their buckets.

It is important to remember the crash
so like the collapse of stock markets
and the slump after euphoria.

It is only worth noting
that there is a knot being untied here,
and things once close are now in separate bowls

and something strangely familiar
I can see out of the corner of my eye
is eagerly climbing the walls.

Christopher Hobday

Man made light work of our removal.
Now he unearths us, pulling away
our ancient blanket with talon-like tools.

Years he spent erasing our name.
Hunting for pleasure, denying
our place on their plate –

our tough as leather
flesh flung to the drooling
snap-jaw of their dogs.

Now they marvel at us in museums.
Bringing their young to study
the redundancy of our wings –

a joke-gift from God, who during
His arduous task of creation
decided to let off some steam,

setting us on an island
where shadows were not feared
and where death came natural,

not a teeth torn, feather shredded
skin sliced annihilation, so when
man clambered from boats

kissing the sand, we waddled
from the shrubbery, squawking
our hello's. Man responded

with chase and spear. It was
then we flapped our frantic wings
but found not height but laughter.

Here is not home. I have watched
the moon curdle in the frozen glare
of my brothers, have heard

children laugh at our crushed thumb
beaks. But I maintain composure,
for in my deep-soil sleep

I have heard the whispering of rebellion
from the unsettled assembly of core
which is soon to begin the great inhale

Vincent Turner

THE DOG SHOOT

Sunday morning and we woke to the pop-pop of guns.
Across the stretch of sand, near the Bedouin village,
a Sharjah soldier had a shot dog by a back leg,
one of the pye dogs that we fed.

There was a whole heap of them, chucked
into an old oil drum on the back of a lorry.
Most were not quite dead. Wet noses
stuck out all uneven, paws paddling the air
as if in safe dreams. The whole drum heaved
like a can of caught worms.

We scampered about the compound
tripping in the sand, fetching dogs in
until the house was packed out with those saved.
Then we pounded after the truck, waving our arms.
My mother fell on the subca track and split
her seventies tight pink pants from seam to seam.

Fiona Owen

The smell lingers,
three months after the floor-shaking thud
when he hared down the stairs shouting, *It's Rafi!*

Flames leapt through the basement grill,
splinters of glass gleamed orange.
You forgot your shoes! she screamed

but he was pulling a man with bloodied legs
clear, as sirens sped towards them;
hoses began to turn the house grey.

She still listens for the child,
for the yell of a girl who slammed doors;
there's only the creak of a fence

against the ceonothus and a thrush
cracking open a snail's shell.

Geraldine Paine

Nurse said
to lose a stone.
I buried it deep
in the garden,
moved house; but
somehow it always
worked its way
back to me. I hid it
in a river, amongst
thousands of others
so it would never
be found

Seeking comfort
for this loss
I began to eat:
I dined on flints
and shingle, wafers
of slate and shale.
Nurse palpated
my heavy heart.
Try and drink more
water, she said.
I went to the river,
drank deeply

Nurse said
to take one of these
whenever I felt
empty – but I was
no longer listening,
I had struck out
for the far shore,
where I could hear
my stone turning
to sand, settling
weightlessly
on the ocean bed

Frances Knight

a rounded head, lizard like
heart shaped olive brown shell
softer on the underside

they had to do it,
a moonless night, a small boat
a single oar to scull

she forages for seaweed and algae
in lagoons by the shore
mates in inlets by the mangroves

no spotted grouper by the landing stage
no grey mullet in the bay
they'd not eaten for days

she returns to the same nesting place
covers the eggs in sand, flings it
round the nest to conceal all trace

water in the lagoon thick with plankton
shoals of tiny fish like jewels
a cloud of diamonds from the oar

she nests at night
the blackness a protection
from frigate bird and boar

sudden thrust of a hook
beneath the curved carapace
desperate flailing flippers

guided by starlight, her hatchlings
move in darkness across the sand
to the safety of the sea

they left it on its back
on the beach overnight

shot it in the morning

    Wisty Thomas

They gather on the flat garage roof
peck at small puddles on the speckled felt,
strutt about a bit, then settle for the treatment –
perfect day for a shower.

Five rose-blushed, mushroom-soft chests,
foie-gras heads, a dab of crème fraiche
on the neck, they plump themselves up then
lean into the breeze;

the technique is to raise one smokey wing,
its underside a vanilla ripple ruched
cotton sail, feathers fluffed to trap the sweet
refreshing raindrops.

After a while the shiver and the shimmy,
shake and fan of the tail, tango-snap
of the head, sharp beak stabbing to extract
unwanted mites.

On other days I complain about their greed,
my colleague offers to bring along an air gun
Five delicious dinners ready for plucking
I almost weaken

but not today.

Clare Dawes

Chanced on in trees by a road,
as if abandoned, an old terrier.

Ramming itself down burrows, rushing
from one dirty hole to another.

As if the only thing it knew to do
was hurt itself and hurt itself again.

Its hare lip, its filthy teeth.
Its shitty coat, the edge of menace

running through its running.
It shrank back, circled, crept up.

We tried to keep our distance,
tried to shoo and shout it off.

It shrank back, circled, crept up,
at last had me cornered

and lifted its head to bite, I thought –
but only looked. And looked.

And in that look, such longing.
Such open, unguarded need.

This world, which cares for nothing,
which teaches such lessons of loss.

This world our only home.

Mark Roper

She had it wrong, the girl who thought
she knew waving from drowning,
could tell the edge of life from its middle,
see shape and bone change to the flat
of ocean. Drowning is the desperate quiet,
the body pinned upright, the lunge
of sea and air.

Those who yell and splash still have time
for speech, to strike a bargain with a wave,
debate the motion of the tides.
Look instead for ones that gaze at you
with blinded eyes, already treading
some internal stair; climbing a ladder
that isn't there.

Rosemary Badcoe

SWIFTS

The common swift: apus apus. Numbers of long distance migrants like the swift are declining at an alarming, accelerating, possibly unsustainable, rate.

Not here this year, lost souls, homes worn away,
handhold to fingertips, like spent pueblos.
They don't die back or hibernate, but cruise
vast distances above the turning world.
July evenings, they side-step, scissor-kick
thin air, etch pen 'n' ink invisible
tattoos. Banshees, dust devils in wet suits,
anchors on skeins of rising light, they're soon
shrill specks in your mind's eye. Time lords, stealth craft
hot wired to while away brief summer nights,
they preen, breed on the wing, use what the wind
blows in to feed, fix nests under house eaves.
Broadcast, they silhouette the urban sky,
shape-shift, in one heartbeat, present and past.

Peter Branson

Two mile tailback, all because
there's a swan in the inside lane, his pale
innocence awkwardly transplanted.
He tenses in wild white panic,
totters and stumbles, stuck, and no one dares
help. The cars drive edgily on.

The ending? Maybe some truck in a hurry
thought he wasn't really worth
the wait, and he's crushed to crimson,
a smear of stained feathers.
Or maybe – *please* – he found his way to the river,
his cygnets, the sheltering willows.

But I still see him, swaying uncertain
like a drunk who's lost his key, alone
in a world of hurtling metal.

Steven Bliss

CONTEMPORARY ART MAY DAMAGE YOUR HEALTH

'Life is never guaranteed to be safe': Ai Weiwei,
Guardian *interview, 18 March 2010*

They're all fired up and painted, ready to party,
spill between fingers, press up between toes,
cling to the soles of shoes, slipping, shifting,
skim along from one end to the other.

We're willing, but the mandarins say *No*.
They fear we might inhale the porcelain dust
as we cavort upon the willing shingle,
picnicking on river crab and buns.

So now a hundred million sunflower seeds
lie raked and still across the Turbine Hall
ankle deep, maybe. We may not touch,
scuff, stuff into pockets, only watch.

The Sunflower Seeds are under house-arrest.

Jenifer Kahawatte

This is his first afternoon with Madame
in her flat above the bookshop, the buses
whining through the drizzle along
Islington High Street. He likes
her colour scheme – bold purple, gold,
everything flickering in the candle-light,
very different from the magnolia anaglypta
and white skirting boards in Theydon Bois
– and the scarlet drapes and Turkish kilim
where a one-eyed ginger cat
regards Madame's whip phlegmatically
as she trails it across his thigh. He likes
the joss sticks dropping ash
onto the floor like insouciant students
though he's less keen on the actual pain –
the bite into the flesh; he slips further
from the room, each lash a descent
into darkness, his skin laid open,
vision blurring and that's when
he realises he's forgotten the Safe Word.
It's a place, yes – some northern town
he visited as a child. He remembers
grit-stone houses under a film of rain,
women in beige with bosoms big enough
to offer shelter and the smell of baking,
a wet dog itching its fur against his legs.
He'd said to Marjorie several times
he'd like to retire somewhere like that,
somewhere with hills, real hills, the light
on them blue as the day went. *Look*,
he whimpers to Madame, *do you think
you could stop that now* – but no,
she's in her stride, a real professional,
and he's so tightly bound, his wrists
chafing on her iron bedstead.
He can feel her breath on his neck, yeasty
and warm as the loaves in the bakery ovens,
swelling and rising to greet the new day.

Catherine Smith

I woke before the bell
in one of the work tents.
Sometimes, after a dream, I still
hear my watch, the splinters
of gold under glass, clicking,
far away as rain on a roof
or rattling trams –

then I can't move until I remember
or he finds me and shakes me until
I remember that I don't need anything
especially not some bourgeois property
unclasped from an exposed wrist, as I kneeled
at a bedside and held someone's hand –

but this morning I get up on duty wide awake
to track a small tent outside the camp
that moves every day, follow a trail of canvas
dragged through sand, inside the perimeter
up to a cypress close to the centre-fire

and that night, over chickpea/soya and bread
I watch the strangers who watch us
through the flames and hear them whisper
in English and German.
One of them has heard about me:
the tall brunette with a broken arm
she says,

but then one of the babies is crying
and any of the babies could be mine,
so I go and feed it as much as I can,
a girl this one, hold her wet cheek
close to my mouth, tell her
I'm all that she needs, stop crying,
everything's fine.

Megan Watkins

We stalked lands
taking air from last breaths,
used sperm from the last Viagra fix,
whilst men lay wizened and stiff
in sun-baked chasms, and children
with bloated bellies clung to women
cracked and creased.

We stole milk
from the squeeze-dried udders
of sad-eyed cattle to feed our babes,
whilst you strapped my lactating breasts,
swollen, engorged and marbled
like the moon.

We flushed water
from behind the last dam,
then queued, portly and proud,
keeping our date for liposuction.
And our smiles – our smiles?

O! our teeth gleam so white.

Eleanor J Vale

RAINDANCE

She hides under her own bones
head hung under the weight of her skull
like a fox on the lawn.

She hides in the hat of her own dreams
tiptoeing under the eaves of shops
in the doorways and malls of the city.

She's under trees. Holding onto
oaks and beeches until the leaves fall
and the rain falls on her eyes
                 falls
                      on
                            her
                                  eyes

Lucy Rutter

Fresh from the ferry on see-sawing ground
they caught me among the containers.

A boy about six and two shades of dirt darker
than either his friend or even his brother,
dressed in the net of a grubby string vest
which swept the floor and concealed his feet.

The tears in their shirts and the dirt were bait
to hook the unwary and weary sailor,
the guise of which I was unable to fit.

I knew that the glint and the wink of light,
the golden glance of a single coin
could dig its hooks in a crowd of eyes
and drown the docks in a shoal of boys.

I gave and I gave and I gave two words
Walung Peso, Walung Peso
hurling the truth across their heads
no money to spare after board and bed.

I saw them again later that night
while hunting the streets for a place to eat,
they slept on a step just out of the rain
their backs to the church and statue of Christ
who gazed on the scene with impassioned eyes.

I like to say I stopped and turned
to place some money beneath one hand.
In truth I paused to snap one shot
the line pulled loose, the fish was lost.

Ben Johnson

He lived on the edge of everything,
clinging with toes and fingertips,
looking down, down at
ordinary people's upturned faces,
pale petals floating
on the pond of normality.
At night in the dark he'd watch
lights flick on in our rooms
but still remained outside,
his wild hair finger-combed to one side
as though constantly
in a high wind. Up there
on his mind's tenth-floor window sill
he looked flattened,
inching along the ledge of life.

For months we tried to talk him down,
to talk him in.
I could have told him: life
runs on ahead without you,
it does that sometimes.
But he wasn't available to listen,
his whole self engaged in holding on.

When at last he fell,
when we found the window
of our effort empty, he'd almost gone,
a dot already dwindling.
There was no point now in calling
after the thin man
striding through the crowd.

    Christine West

You arrive at dawn – isolated
buildings cast grey shadows
like loitering ghosts.

You conceal yourself in a porch corner.
Rain from a gutter beats a syncopated pattern.
The rutted road is a running stream
washing away yesterday's heat –
the smell of damp earth reminds you
of wet wool – a blanket removed
from your grip on comfort.

Jangling keys wake you.
A mackintoshed figure stoops,
holds out his hands,
    smiles,
shrugs at the rain.

Some things we cannot predict.

You follow him into the café,
with its rainbow painted wall.

Patricia Griffin

for Diana Hendry

It's the property of angels, I've been told,
To arrive without warning, when needed most.

So you, on an April Monday when trains were bad,
Suddenly. Phoning the day before, you'd heard
My silence, how I couldn't speak; had rung again
To tell me when to meet you. Sudden as magic.

Smoke-scented, light out of light into dark,
Behind you a long day's journey into night,
Our night.
           Undismayed, equable, strong Diana,
You gave us four days of you. In your shining,
Our crippled courage shook itself, and tried again.

What angels do, you did – hope in despair,
Strength in weakness – all the usual chores;
And soup, and shopping. How do you thank
Angels? It was Easter, season of surprising things.

It's just I'd never thought of you before as having wings.

R V Bailey

Winter of floods – winter of broken banks
and radio warnings and me running
down the road with the pushchair screaming
and a cloud helicoptering low behind me.

Remember even the genteel Cherwell
bursting, the Isis brimming, swelling under
its muddy meniscus like a body rolling
in sleep in a blanket? The times you came home

to find the armchairs floating, the carpet
a quicksand, the tables at unprecedented levels,
the baby awash in his Moses basket and me
bailing madly as he rose to the ceiling?

Yet here we all are, no worse than muddy, and look –
the hills emerging, exactly the same, casual as knees.

Kate Clanchy

DEATH BY LIGHTNING

I left you in the house, your eyes on me,
suffering from a relative of grief,
took myself from here to the neighbouring village.
I don't usually walk, preferring donkey or moped,
but neither could fare in the weather:
rain slopped from eaves
turning the streets to streams.
Thin fish lost their bearings and followed
to be found tomorrow, breathless,
heads in the railings.
I doubt they knew anything about it,
sent to sleep by strange air lifting their scales.
Rain was in my neck, my boots were buckets,
sky a marbling of dark and unfamiliar faces,
clouds deep as difficult ideas, luminous at their edges.
Light cleaved the sky. I counted and wasn't disappointed
by the sound of a giant piano dropped

onto a collection of empty cauldrons.
I smiled: the sky was furious for me
so I might stay inside the cupboard of my head.
But soon the water overcame, tipping
from flat roofs, stabbing from the arms of lampposts.
Paving slabs lifted to expose whole villages
of slugs and toads.
The sea, two miles away, suggested itself on the wind.
Light revealed a shape at the graveyard gate: a woman under
a yew older than landscape. Room for two. I joined her,
politely distant, staring at the knots and carvings in the trunk:
tracks of every death that's marked elsewhere in stone,
hems of marriages leaving the gate, home for ivy,
sheets of frost and mushrooms shelving out like flesh.
The woman watched the rain as if to concentrate
on just one drop and shuddered when the thunder
spread its voice above the leaves.
She was not beautiful.
She didn't hold her body supple as an animal.
I could not name her type of smile.
Later, I learned she felt the shock in her foot;
shared what I cannot remember.
I looked up through the branches holding
tight their fists of leaves.
I have that image stencilled on my eyelids.
I smelled that metal in the air and tasted
nothing.
You know, if you watch anything through flashes
of lightning, it appears suspended
as if life were frame after frame and never moving.
I was senseless: a snapshot of myself under a canopy.
I'm still here, now in the living room
where we question each other.
I didn't replay memories or gain an answer,
but I've read the best stuff has the power
to take off the top of your head.
You've changed, though you never left this room.
Every day you run your hands over
the root-system printed red on my chest
and in the dark part of your eye
I detect a storm.

Abi Curtis

We exchange the warm
steam of silence for this:
gales of flaying rain,
huddles of sheep,

stranded islands
where white horses rear
and rear against the rocks.
A thunderous, shattered sea.

Storm force ten, rising.
And rising.
Only stone stands.
Our footprints are swept out

from under our feet
and flung back
in our faces. Grit.
The blade of the north wind

is sharpened and polished
and we are balanced on it.

Janice Fixter

For three days the wind raked the world with its
fists; and while the compliant staggered and
stayed on its feet, the unbending shuddered
till it cracked and crumbled onto its knees.

A horde of horsemen rode across the sky,
so many it took three days for them to
pass. The earth trembled, dancing like clods in
a riddle; and the thunder of their hooves
struck sparks from the hilltops and the lash of
their rain raised welts on our heads and shoulders.

On the third day the storm subsided and
the birch trees sprang and sang silver in the
sunlight; the gorse swelled green with a plumpness
of bud and the corn grew lush in the fields.

And we looked upon the world and saw that
it was good – we were alive, my wife's hands
lay clasped across her swollen belly and
my two boys ran the hill on sturdy limbs –
never minding that our roof-tree lay snapped
and splintered on a broken back of stones.

Andrew McCallum

The auspices are uncertain,
rain threatens in the east –
a bit black over Bill's mother's
as they say in these parts –
although sunlight creeps in
from the west in spite
of the banks of cloud.

We can take nothing for granted here
even the seasons have stalled,
the summer's swifts still circling the house,
the annuals reluctant to fade –
picnics in October, and thickening grass.

We forget the earth is alive beneath our feet,
will not die or even rest
according to the clocks we make.
Prediction is a lost art.

Put two and two together
and we get nothing but conjecture, at best,
the chance that chaos
was all the time the answer.

Although there's always hope,
like seeing the rain, drifting now
from the east, falling on *Bill's mother's*
as we guessed it would.

  Derrick Buttress

In Dominica, an earthquake cracked
Roger's home like a walnut.
His wife's omelette pan skipped off the stove,
their bed hopped the floor, chairs
pirouetted into shaking walls.
But cotted snug in a box for their breakfast:
half a dozen eggs, unbroken.

Visiting his mother in Grenada,
a hurricane peeled her house like an orange,
the winds stacked roofs, turned
tamarind trees into mops, uprooted
nutmeg plantations but left the glass
of his daughter's portrait a smooth,
unrippled ocean.

Half-submerged in New Orleans, Roger's shoes
walked in pairs on water. Tables arked,
chairs waded out the doors
and dead rats trailed the apartment stairs,
while his daughter's dress
hung freshly pressed on her bedroom door:
dry and pink with flowers.

Sarah James

SLOW BURN

No need to run when he crosses the savannah,
where there are no roads, no buses to catch,
no commuter trains and few possessions
but when a storm threatens, he clambers
onto his corrugated roof to anchor
three worn tyres onto the rusting metal
for he's never heard of a car being struck
by lightning as it speeds along on rubber-shod wheels

Angela Croft

My mother used to hide
under the bed during thunder storms.
She passed some of her fear on to me.
Being afraid of electricity
bolting down from the sky
sounds reasonable enough.

She was already part the way down Alzheimer's path
when Hurricane Charley blew through.
She hadn't the imagination to be frightened,
so she and my dad sat in the family room
as if it were a normal day –
that room with the big picture window.

When they were in the eye of the storm
they went outside into perfect stillness
to see the first half of the damage.
I try to imagine them, both calm,
my dad so he wouldn't frighten my mom,
and she, used to things not making sense by then.

Then they went back inside
to sit out the wind's second onslaught,
from the opposite direction.

   Connie Ramsay Bott

for Rachel Chambers

So – as I argued about the prices of laptops,
worried about not doing any work
and cleared the desk, made pots of tea for two,
picnicked near Brecon – you huddled up a gorge
in Ladakh, as flash floods thundered away
five of your companions, slower to run,
so drowned behind you. And I've no right to say

what this is like. I'm silent, nod, half-smile.
You speak so calmly: of digging with your hands
to stay alive; that constant smash of water;
dodging rock-fall, *like a computer game;*
four comfortless nights with death, wanting your mum.
But jetlagged tonight, between my wife and me,

you sipped our gin, dropped earrings down a chair,
destroyed a glass, spilled bags across the floor,
your same dishevelled self. And how you survived
is a mystery to us, we cannot joke.
Nor dare we think why perhaps we love you more.
And now we've gone to bed. My note reads just:

It's good to have you back. Words can fail.
But such things, Rachel, are coal for poetry,
so here we are. Because there *you* are now
in the next-door room, curled up on the sofa
yet again, my friend. It's old, but plush, and deep,
and holds you like a seed squat in a palm
as rain jitters down the window while you sleep.

Rory Waterman

Remember the place
I showed you, the place
where the turtles lay eggs at full moon.

Remember my father – stilt-fisherman –
silhouetted *like a black flamingo,* you said,
dipping its beak in the shimmering sea.

You came on the ramshackle train
from Colombo, past the fish market at Galle
teaming with lobster, tuna, prawns

via Unawatuna where rainbow coral shone
through a glass-bottomed boat
to Weligama,with its temple to Buddha

and my uncle's guesthouse where we chewed
betel together, ate hoppers and monkfish.
I told you our stories, sang you our songs there.

Remember the day the sea breathed
a huge inward breath and the waves
peeled back revealing the reef…

the day the animals sensed a change in the air,
ran into the mangrove, monkeys chattering,
old Basnayake's elephants trumpeting

as the hump in the ocean turned
into a mountain of water rushing towards us.
No-one had warned us!

I ran up the beach, racing inland
past the coconut palms and
the railway track crossing – the roar in my ears –

to the safe arms of Buddha. I clung to his neck
as the water rose and the bodies floated in
from the train that was hit by the force of the water.

The same train you left on, that day in December.*

Vivienne Tregenza

* *Boxing Day 2004*

The wind blew from four directions,
snowflakes streamed diagonally across,
crevasses cracked open before us,
minor slab avalanches swept under us,
misunderstandings arose between us,
we shouted unheard abuse…
once a Japanese rope held me
but two of its three strands had loosed!

My past flashed before me, like they say it does,
but with the unreality of events read about.
Sorry only that everything was at an end
I did not dread the moment of death.
Just as my hand clung to the rope
secured by the piton, so my mind
clung to familiar pieties
afraid that sanity would be swept away.

We kicked our crampons and swung our axes,
concentrating on the mechanics of persistence.
Suddenly we could see the glacier
appear and disappear below our feet.
The flame that had flickered within
which the storm could not wholly extinguish
steadied to burn more firmly, so that
smiles threatened to crack our masks of ice.

All that we had salvaged from the attempt
was ourselves. When we saw our porters
it was our happiest human encounter
and we embraced them. They brought us
three little blue flowers from the moraine,
which came to stand for our deliverance.
From that moment we had a new
measure for our lives: before and after.

John Killick

1943

Up the Ton Mawr Road, uncharted night,
where snow has buried the trees
and the moon lights up the old car
that can't climb any further. The air
in the hills is barren, cold. Ice devours
everything even a couple walking
against night. The sheep are bleating
ignored by the shepherd who listens elsewhere,
boils kettles, piles up the towels.

Two figures struggle on to the croft.
They falter, almost turn back,
on this night where the air consumes even
the most human of souls. The doctor's wife
knows what she has to do, make the tea,
hold the woman, time the contractions.
Doctor and shepherd wait for a whisky,
she wonders about love on a night like this.
The screams, the cries, the joy, the pain and ice.

Wendy French

DO'S AND DON'T

This product should reach you in perfect working order,
but please examine carefully
and acquaint yourself with the detail of the smaller parts.

Coming in a variety of shapes and sizes,
although starting small, it will progressively expand
to reach its optimum width and height.

It is important to take particular care
of all internal mechanisms and circuitry
encased within the outer protective skin.

This comes in several different shades
but, although elastic and flexible,
is itself quite sensitive and vulnerable.

Once ejected from the parent body,
it will need to be disconnected and started-up
(sometimes requiring a firm initial slap).

It should then locate and operate
all external doors or hatches
which are designed for putting-out and taking-in.

If not functioning correctly,
it will automatically sound an alarm.
This will increase to maximum volume,

requiring careful handling
to ensure satisfactory shut down.
It will now need regular re-fuelling, at first on demand.

Make sure all legs and grabs are in full working order.
It should start to explore edges:
shadow and light, smiles and frowns,

boxes of every sort, until its reserves of energy run down.
Then it should automatically switch to sleep mode
(if not, turn on its front).

Finally, having explored everything within view or reach,
it may want to become free-standing and move around.
It should quickly learn to respond to adverse circumstances

but will also need to react to request and demand.
Though there are no guarantees
(it is a gift, after all, not a purchase!)

it is expected to last well into double figures
and has been known to last beyond.
It is hoped that you will be

completely satisfied with this product,
but beware there is a risk of attachment
and inexplicable functions such as love.

Phil Barrett

The cold snap was sudden in '78,
and you had me, a coatless infant,
and no money to spare. I doubt
it was your aim to save the sixteen
glass litre bottles in the closet
for a moment such as this. But
there they were, treasure discounted
behind Christmas decorations.

On hands and knees, you crawled
through a forest of pine-scented boxes,
one of pokey plastic pine needles
that would never know decay
and poinsettia blossoms bedecked
in glitter, as drenched in iridescence as
the mermaids we watched beneath
a glass-bottomed boat in Silver Springs,
and retrieved what would be redeemed
for nine dollars and change.

How wise it seemed then,
when times were tight, to hold
this little bit back, a blessed boon
of redeemable glass from the summer
you, still a child yourself,
drank Coke
on your lunch breaks, when you could
come home from laying carpet
in remodelled apartments, none complete
with air conditioning.

Jamie A Hughes

Jodie and Mary were born in St Mary's Hospital,
Manchester, August 2000

Two babies in one, fused
at the spine, joined at the abdomen,
their limbs ram-
rodded at right angles.

And then a second trick –
in less than a day, the surgeons
separate bone and flesh, a body
from its heart and magically

the girls are free, apart
for an instant
before one is able to live
without having to pump blood

for her sister, breathe
for her sister, drag
her sister's body.
Through little tricks she will

survive. The first: to ease
the strain of being alone,
one cold mirror propped
in her cot, beside her.

Mara Bergman

A Vietnamese water-colour:
mother shaded by conical hat,
boat-pole poised against the sky,
daughter's water-lily face,
begging me to take a ride.

As mother parts muddy shallows,
Nee practises her English –
together we sing 'Jingle Bells',
her pure tones
skipping across oil-smooth water.

A flock of houseboats
bumps hindquarters
in our wake.
Nee's moonface beauty clouds:
Those are poor people, she says.
We live on that small island –
since the fire
burnt our house.

She lifts a silken screen of hair
to show me the scar –
her apocalypse.

Nee's progress
on a sea of chance
flows with the English language,
but I am dumbed
by the weight
of dollars in my purse.

That evening,
as I sit in Hoi An's streets
of coloured lanterns,
she passes,
graces me with more smiles,
spooling away
on a finely spun thread.

When I think of her now,
she's enclosed in a silk lantern,
lit by her luminous face,
poling to a new life,
at the beat
of that generous heart.

Margaret Eddershaw

IN PRAISE OF THE CHILDREN WHO SELL SCARVES AT ANGKOR WAT

They celebrate the divinity of free enterprise,
for though they travel in flocks, each,
like a homing pigeon, represents himself.

Their teeth have the sharpness of Piranhas
or vampires, the better to bleed us dry
of compassion and currency, but their arms

are filled with rainbows. They coo and croon
their wares, remind us of hope –
you buy my scarf – one dollar? They do not accept

no, or understand it. They terrify us into random acts
of kindness, and sated with scarves we are each,
in turn, satisfied with the deal. They honour us

with their attention, *you come back soon?*
and we shower them with bills,
grateful for their beauty.

Wendy Klein

That shock of first-drawn breath.
Love leaking, like milk.
Devotion, new-born and fierce.
Slick infant laid to breast
marks the passage from kitten to crone.
She has survived the rite and earned her tiger stripes
among the daughters of Eve.
She takes her place before legions of mothers,
and the mothers of mothers.
Rank upon rank of them,
a terracotta army shrouded in mist.
Old wives with tales for the telling,
and old ways of knowing.
And wise words to impart,
like amulets,
to protect the heart.

Sandra Ireland

Zenaida macroura

I want to tell my son everything –
how home was a red-wing black bird call,
a sound like a roller blind pulled up suddenly,
in the field behind Virginia's house
where you look up and see the pearl-grey sky wide and
empty in the morning by the stand of giant pines,
like a mountain of green on great, fat trunks,
storm dark, smelling of pitch,
and below them russet needles
weave a thick mat where your feet sink and
pineapple-size cones emerge.
Mourning doves cry, cry, cry high above
and you could too – but you don't
with your sneakers full of foxtails and wild oat stickers
crunching through dry grass and brittle mustard plants.
You aren't running away – but could you?
And ahead, a horse whinnies by the electric fence where
sometimes the boys dare each other to pee on the current
and yes it hurts, but that's not real pain
because it goes away.

My big, giant boy –
my grown-up son who knows so much,
if I could take you back to when you were seven
and we could buy ice-cream and you would tell me
just everything and I could embrace away anything,
just hug away every bad thing, would I be
hugging for England?
for California? or maybe
just for me?
But neither of us can go back.
They've cut down the trees
and there is more to this old home story than
pretty birds, though I'm sure the mourning doves
still call from some new suburban fence
and it sounds like they say
Don't cry, cry, cry, cry.

Mark Holihan

She got used to the birds
flying around the house

except for the days
when their cawing filtered
through the floorboards

and even the dog was afraid.

When friends or relations came
the birds disappeared through the windows
and waited on the roof top
or under the eaves.

One day the cawing stopped.

The birds settled in the silence
like a big black cloud.

In her bedroom she built a cage
and the birds flew in
one by one.

Weeks later she returned from school
found her mother and father
in the kitchen – kissing.

From her room she could hear
the flutter of a million tiny wings.

The door opened and the birds
glided through the house

weightless and blue.

Maggie Sawkins

I know that I am thirty years too late to travel down that valley
of other-skin, to imagine you bent over, biting your lip,
crying out for your Dad, who would have fixed it all;
would have taught Grandpa how to be a man,
would have shocked your Mum into listening out and peering
behind closed doors. It is too late to go back to the year
before the beatings, or hold your hand on the day
of your Father's funeral as you ask: Where have all the men gone?

Sometimes when you lean to turn the light off, I catch a glimpse
of the lines of scars in the grooves of your lower back
before the darkness stamps them out. You seem surprised
that they are visible, or that I feel for that boy as I do –
you tell me he is not you, he is not you, those scars no longer
      wake you,
only the feel of my fingers, in the half light, tracing the arc
      of time.

   Dorothy Fryd

It was almost dark when we got there
I was not invited to speak
nor asked how the train had been

Beneath glowering streetlights
                              my driver's neck
rigid beneath her permanent wave
gloved hands firm at ten to two

Suitcase quiet beside me in the back
my nametag
                written by Dad
at the far-off beginning of the day

At a house with a pretty name
she parked in the only pool of light
                              and left me
to find the back door
in the thickening dark

There was a glass of cold milk
another journey up a shadowed stair
a bed I didn't know, where
I tucked the nametag
                    beneath my pillow
                              and held on tight.

Vanessa Gebbie

Stopped off to see my old school.
Didn't go in, stood outside
and looked up at the windows
of the stark, straight-up-and-down
dormitory where we learned
never to crack. And, mended
now, the tall narrow window
next to it, with, my story
insists, a fat waterpipe
crossing the wall inside it –

from which, one winter morning
in the early 1950s, I
monkey-hung, while the voice
of our cold tap deepened, and, flea-
picking, dangling, swinging, swung
slap back against our iced-up
bathroom window. And through it.
The smack of splintering glass,
the crashing, tinkling fall, down
to the Headmaster's rosebed –

I hear it happen now. What
can't totally have happened
is a flying body which,
as the story grows, swung out
clean through the jagged man-sized
hole and clean back in again.
The miracle is we came
through so unhurt, if unhurt
is when bodies conjure blood
to hide the mouths of their wounds.

Hubert Moore

Wild garlic is coming into flower
where the hens used to scratch.
All the grey houses are open
to the wind. We visit the schoolroom
with its desks and china inkwells,
the coatless pegs, marked with a name.

Beside each faded name
is a bird, a butterfly or a flower.
Vera remembers filling the inkwells.
Some days a regular dip and scratch
was the only sound in the schoolroom.
Teacher would let the door stand open

and use the pole in the corner to open
the windows. 'Mind you use the right name.'
She'd tap round the schoolroom.
'Not that! Whoever heard of a flower
called blue buttons?' No-one dared scratch
out a word. They jabbed at their inkwells.

Summer insects drowned in these inkwells.
Hair clogged nibs. An open
vowel became a shiny blob. Scratch!
'Us has a new baby. Her name
is Violet, same as the flower.'
They could hear her from the schoolroom.

That winter the stove in the schoolroom
seized. Ink froze in the inkwells
and before the last intricate frost flower
melted on glass, their minds shivered open
to ice-bound forests, wastes without a name,
cold queens who used their fingernails to scratch

out hearts. Then, at a stroke, the scratch
of a signature emptied their schoolroom.
The army needed it to shell. Name
after name, straight from these inkwells
was blotted dry in the books that lie open.
One page is marked by a khaki-coloured flower.

Only mice scratch when the guns stop rattling inkwells
in the country schoolroom. On the few days it's open
remember them by name – a bird, a butterfly or a flower.

Ruth Smith

IDIOMS FOR SURVIVAL

My parents lived through
They lived through
Like the context was a container
Like a cracked jug
Or a green tattered net

And like hot milk
Or a redbellied dace
They lived through
Like living was dripping, was seeping
Like living was writhing free.

Kyrill Potapov

'I wish I had finished it.'
Diary entry made by Anne while writing Agnes Grey

I

In childhood's lonely kingdom it was our comfort
to be each a queen in a presumptive sisterhood.

We broke free in sorties like the wilder goddesses,
reeling from the baize table, from Father's scattered homilies

through the cold parlour, trampling over, sidling round
memories of Mother thrown in our path like stitchery

(kerchiefs of domesticity we would not take up);
tip-toed past the brother whose untidy black body

sprawled in the schoolroom in a masculine knot
while his tongue thickly practised classical verse;

so we found out the moors, our wind-dizzy playground,
where we fluttered like kites as our minds learned to soar.

II

Years later, when the moors – like everywhere – had become
criss-crossed with failures like narrow paths much travelled,

we were blown home again, blown together by winters,
and we sat sighing or smiling and tilting our shadows

across snow-blank pages, where with deliberate black strokes
we turned daydreams to architecture, but broken like monasteries –

or like ourselves in age and in childlessness. Emily
bequeathed us all a labyrinth, where circular winds

chased down the generations, and predatory eyes
saw casements slam down on our bleeding ghosts;

Charlotte took local scarecrows, favoured the limp males,
and stuffed them full of bitter-sweetness as Christmas puddings –

to store in our doll's house of delusions concerning the rich.
I was the youngest. Pale-faced, I tried to echo their truth

in my stories, while my sick days closed about me like stones...
Sisters: closest to silence, I spoke only to mark the end.

Alan Gleave

THE SCRABBLE BOX

Brown, shabby, mended with Sellotape,
still here, four houses and fifty years on.
New tiles, yes, for those that mysteriously disappeared,
new racks, to replace those chewed by the puppy Rex.
No new rules required.
We knew those by heart.

And shabby? That's not the word
for such an elegant, stylish antique,
with a pedigree no new set could match
(in a corner of the box there's still 21/-,
the price I paid at Smith's, in the Earl's Court Road).

The other corner shows triumphant scores,
words that defeated all challenges.
(*Dad, there's no such word as 'helicol',
'machair' or 'zymotic'.*)
But there always was, and here are the scores to prove it –
eleven, fourteen, and twenty-two
(or rather sixty-six for a triple word score).

I'll keep that game; others more easily won
might give a higher score but this old box held fun,
and best of all it has survived the past
bringing back days when we were young.

Val Doyle

I thought I had caught it once,
darting into the wave
as we walked along old concrete sea walls
while the sea was the same colour as the rain clouds,
grey foam that had leaked through new trainers.
I grabbed at it, salt water on my hair
turning the French braids my Grandmother had worked
so hard on, into frizzy, pointed plaits with wet ends.
Hands in my pockets,
I thought I had it, wrapped around my little finger;
thought I could bring it, the air, the sand, the water
back to London with me, that it would survive in the city,
but the city's rain watered it down
until the last drop evaporated and it was gone again.

For years its deep pull,
the tide washing up my nose
and hooking me like the fish, a sharp and sure pull,
was forgotten and lost.
Curious, I searched it out like an addiction,
sat with my feet in it,
the drug seeping into my pores.
I had it all – the dolphins one metre away on Australian sands,
starfishes stuck on boating lakes in the North Sea.
Bittersweet saltwater kisses; tide soaked beaches.

When I was thirteen I saw someone painting
over the single glazed windows that encased
us children on this ward. A vivid blue outlined in black,
fishes composed of circles and triangles.
Every morning I had a sunny blue on my face
I could almost touch it,
even while they took a needle out and stole
blood from children – my own deep red sea.

Eleanor Ward

Mine was the first voice you heard
singing Bob Marley and The Stones' 'Angie'
as you swam in my womb –

you had no choice but to listen
trapped within my skin!
But you were born on a blue wave
where whales and dolphins played
ushered to me with the grace
of a thousand centuries
the slice of knives
the red wash of a Phagwah day.

Music flowed in your blood
echoes of a grand-father playing guitar
on a trans-Atlantic doorstep
tuned your violin, fleshed the spirituals
your English voice now frames so perfectly.
Look at you, head up
those notes falling from your lips
as deep as the oceans crossed by the ships
of harmonies from that day to this.

Myths are woven of passages such as these.

   Maggie Harris

10

Between us we've spent
a hundred and fifty years
on this blue planet,
my mother, my daughter and I,
who've come together
in the postage stamp garden
of my childhood home
to gaze into the darkest reaches
of this clear March night
at a moon made strangely local,
contours clear as the chimneys
on next door's roof, but
rendered unfamiliar
by their ruddy hue,
like some hapless worthy
unaccustomed to the sauce.
And our three worlds spin as one,
three generations reduced
to Bogie's hill of beans
by the dimensions of the night.

They can claim a kinship
with the moon that I'm denied,
but for one tiny moment
the mystery they share
is diminished by the wonder
that is mine as much as theirs.

   Jeremy Page

Some black holes have a ring of x-rays and visible light surrounding them.

Nothing but dark, I said
as I drew our curtains on the darkness
of the birch tree and the robin singing
a snatch of late song,

and yet light all round.
And you understanding. The paradox
of light and dark, a black hole
and a ring of light,

in the space between teacups at ease
on the table and pyracantha
scratching the window beyond
as the wind blew.

Now on a small hill, that place
of wind and silence, the silence
of futures… trees
cut off distances.

Stones, gravestones are master there.
But arriving home I take up that book
of Chinese art, your inscription *A trillion
kisses forever.*

I turn the pages, find the vase with peaches
showing flowers and fruit together,
as in that paradise where peach blossom
lasted for ever.

Irrelevant paradise? But I read
again your inscription: *Perhaps this
is a kind of heaven, the warmth of feeling
and memory,*

light circling a possessed absence.

   Daphne Gloag

Fallen though a crowd of hallelujahs,
this fragment of my soul catches
between one breath
and the next.

No bigger than a thumbnail with a
rainbow and a space of sky
above a hill,
hanging there

to be picked off by some returning dove
off course over infinity
in which your ark
has foundered.

Moyra Tourlamain

LIGHT

I climb into the boat, alone.
Directed by a compass in my heart
To reflect on others who recoiled when
You, sundazzled, dived from yourself
Into an empty space. Exploring the navy
Blue of unmapped countries.

I see only deep waters' flares.
When my senses are wayward
I return, watching thin waves,
See light that lingers, then
Vanishes (in ordinary things)
Like sparks without trace.

One day I'll see an image
Of your boat, with its sails
Torn heading for the shoreline.

Elly Niland

A softening of light; hedgerows rank with stalk, seedheads, curving
bramble, whizening leaves.
Hillsides rust.
By the path, fungi, tiny fists, flesh-brown,
puncture the wet turf. Along power lines
starlings mass, a string of black beads.

All signal summer's passing.

I thought of those old saints, scholars,
faith's hard diamond denying flesh's frailties,
the scourge of gales across this sea-locked land,
rain seeping through bleak cell walls.

A decayed palace is witness to temporal power.

Yet a stroll away, beyond the small, stone-hedged fields,
high cliffs, smooth as slate,
dismiss waves' fury. Beyond, a shimmering sea,
its mirrored sky broken by promontories, islands,
submerged dragons of jagged rock.

Below, across a cove, a seal, dark shadow,
sensuously surfs the shallows.

Colin Speakman

Birdsong melded
with forest fragrance,

butterflies danced
the exuberance of life

while I sipped
Chateau Le Touron,
Monbazillac.

I basked
in the warm glow
of good fortune

as a gentle breeze
blew wispy cloud
across a painter's sky

and then she appeared
with her soft,
Mediterranean eyes

and the je ne sais quoi
of her Gallic mystique,

and reality froze
as she sang
with her angel's voice,
Bonjour, Monsieur!

My mind flashed
across 50 years
to a thousand falters

that had brought me
to this moment,
in this paradise,
on this Earth.

Naturellement, I replied,
Oui, bonnie lass:
a very good day!

  Michael James Treacy

Taken from 'Arundel'

Whatever keeps us going
keeps us together. The
ring on this ring-finger
as wife to a labourer,

gilded gold like an
undying sun. Colossal
life-giver set with a
stone; sets in a sky above

my children. Birthed.
They'd pop like dry pods
open into the wilderness;
would walk two-footed

on hot dirt
as my husband, scoping
the skyline for
signs of habitation

returns with the promise
of a language we could
both lay upon. The
path to Mount Hopeless

disintegrates around
the south plain stretch
into the inland sea
it was always meant to be,

and I, shading the lilac
underlined cloud cover
from a kid's brow, press
out to the desert edge

elongated against every
speck of sand. So sorry
for the drag of us. That
we root down. *Detach!* We,

the unrestless offshoots
of a simpler world. And you,
drunk; half-dead, hush up for
the Eden we should've found.

Simon Everett

It
Was
Midnight
when France
was a 100 kilometers
Behind

At
The border
There had been three women
From a jazz quartet
        Tightening
A grave marker
To the roof
Rack

At
Dawn
There will be
Hot air balloons over
Lucerne

From
Antarctica
No one will
Notice

silent lotus

A cello,
Plangent echo from the well of memory,
And I see her once more;
White arms in the fountain of youth
spray us with gold coins of sunlight:
in the piazza, *La passegiata*.
Lovers murmur again,
families argue and laugh,
in the evening's shade;
and constantly, the chime of church bells.

Now I sit on my steps
the wind sifting my hair
and only an old stray dog,
bumping her three legs over the cobbles towards me,
for company.

To find me, halt the car
at the end of the road, cross
the rickety old bridge on foot:
(look down, if you dare, in the ravine,
at the erosion of centuries).
Only thirty people here now:
all old, left here to die.

Etruscan boys and girls played here once,
before the sober soldiers of the Eagle
sacked the place and brought a kind of peace.
The city thrived later –
you saw the Medici symbols over the gate?
Then other Jackboots came:
over there – the bullet holes where they shot the men
and boys – even the priest –
when I was a prisoner in a cold land.
Tourists still come here (that's one
on the cello). They call this
The Dead City. But we shall die first –
the town will remain as you find it.

Derek Score

I don't remember what it was that set us off,
exploding in the silent space, bent double with laughter,
ignoring the attendant with the missing button who watched
as mother and daughter squealed and shook, told us there was no
accounting for taste. I do remember it looked like a field.
I remember not thinking of what might lie beneath its surface.

And then the puzzled frown on my father's face
turned to hurt as my mother and I continued to scoff
at his choice of outing, drowned his talk of felled
forests and prehistoric graves with our laughter,
gasping and heaving and spluttering, then watching
as he walked away, seeking but finding no

trace of the expected remains. Did he know
our sobs and snorts were less a slap in the face
than a desire to claim a rare shared ground? Each of us
        always watching
for a chance to destabilise the family triangle, to see off
the weakest side, using mockery and laughter
to rock confidence, to unlevel the field.

Or were we just laughing at a man in a field
searching for the meaning of life among the dead? I know
it comforted him to think that four thousand years after
graves were dug and bodies buried, bones stripped bare, faces
long forgotten, angry gods appeased by offerings,
here we stood, survivors of the human race. Watching

the birds flying from tree to ancient tree, watching
the wind still stirring the branches, in this field
we endured. It was his offer
of hope, a hymn to human resilience. No
need to think of individual loss, to face
the emptiness. So why our laughter?

I think now that our sobs and snorts of laughter
were our bid to hold the future at bay: the night-long watch,
the silent waiting room, the blank faces
of strangers, the almost field
studded with neat stones stretching into a no
man's land, the slow walk away, the wake, the send-off…

I wish I saw no need to mine this surface, to question this laughter.
But I can't back off – even though no
one else is left to watch. Why can't a field be just a field?

Vicky Wilson

*Grimes Graves: despite its name, the Neolithic site is not a burial ground
but an ancient flint mine.*

AT BRAMPTON WOOD

No snowdrops, nothing
other than the click
of dry sticks against

each other and the sun
blossoming on the grey
bark of oak.

My mother holds my arm
as we walk
the ride, then read

of how this goes back
to the ice age,
something unchanged, while

all around the roads
were cut. People going
places, and this place

simply staying unmoved.

John Greening

Last light. The shadow falls across the wall
where sunlight flickers its own graffiti
over graffiti's air-brushed promise
Gary wil allways luv Denise xx.
Stone kisses caress but the flinty kiss
of a sated lover transported me and nothing
remained but to move to some other dance.

Empty coal trains clattered the night
Snow clouds hung yellow over a river
leaked with light: passing barges discharged oil
that streaked her blonde hair, glossed lips,
swollen but not from kisses, and rimmed nails
that crazed a bare back all New Year's day when we
remained to move to some other dance.

That summer rain slashed tenements of gulls
that wreathed every pitch and pot of houses
without guests. Pensioners slacked by a dun sea
under an ugly sky. Each clump of rocks the hunch
of her back as I crabbed sand between bare toes,
drew guilt close as a caul around what sadness
remained before moving onto some other dance.

Europe misted memory. A thumb primed at 90 degrees
made lorries shudder dust on mountain roads
where old currency – breasts half tamed in a halter top,
his seed, prolific as pomegranates' –
bartered in the humming dawn and words –
whose words? in which language? – told that despair
remained: had moved into some other dance.

But some languages are not for sharing
so we skimmed countries silently, pointed
out stone and rocky places, avoided
burst tyres, shattered headlights. Visa-less,
India stayed unvisited – but what visa grants
safe passage from memory? – Albania, closed,
remained so as we moved from each other's dance.

Alone, all roads became cross-roads. Each road
a country: each country merely a road.
Yet still the body moved till gradually
Greece beckoned, offered sheep's eyes and Matala stew –
wild onions, grasses, herbs strewn amongst bones
left by lepers before travellers came,
remained, then moved on to some other dance.

If history lies in ancient remains
what history remains in ancient lies?
Leave historians to screen, carbon date,
determine what is to be determined,
a scream, unseen, unheard, terminates
more than one life: this you should know before
you air-brush our graffiti, take my hand
and move these remains in some other dance.

Ruth O'Callaghan

TV FOOTAGE

The interview is always startling: Bets –
two days before her death – bird-like, bright-eyed,
dressed in collared orange knit with pearls,
and concealed in a black belt, her bag
of morphine. She speaks about an hour
with breaks for ice to suck, or to listen
to a question posed about New Zealand
and the sunlit house in which we see her
pillowed in her armchair, a sheepskin throw
behind her, her sky-blue coffin lying open
on the floor. Never-mind the years
in Indonesia, her wartime Holland, the trauma
of departures, or the closing century.
On television they showed the house and asked her
how much she minded talking about death.

Joan Michelson

It's not in my own house
I want to live,
nor in the lighthouse in the bay.

It's not in London
where I lost my soul, nor will I find it
in Paris or Rome.

It's not silence or thought I fear,
nor shadows on the move
in quiet summer-timey St Petersburg.

There's no city in the world
where I'll hear a true word

nor in Outer Space
will I find an un-named star.

It's not through this door
I'll find all I ever desired

nor on this page
will I read my own name.

It isn't in Stornaway
where I'll find Michelangelo's first-ever painting,

I'll have to look elsewhere for that,
and for all of the above.

It's not in an ancient library
where I'll learn to bear the weight of learning,

nor will I find the bread of life
in a bakery –

but one day I'll find a song
on the tip of my tongue

ready and waiting to be sung,
that song knows where it belongs.

Penelope Shuttle

Shanta Acharya was born in India, educated at Oxford and Harvard, lives in London. She is an internationally published poet and her fifth collection is *Dreams That Spell The Light* (Arc Publications, 2010). www.shantaacharya.com. **Patience Agbabi** is a Fellow in Creative Writing at Oxford Brookes University and the author of *Transformatrix* and *Bloodshot Monochrome*. She is currently producing a contemporary version of *The Canterbury Tales*. **Moira Andrew**: born and educated in Scotland, ex-teacher and lecturer, children's poet and author of books for teachers. She has three collections and a new book, *Firebird*, due from Indigo Dreams in 2012. www.moiraandrew. com. **Nnorom Azuonye** is Founder & Administrator of Sentinel Poetry Movement, Administrator of Excel for Charity International Writing Competitions Series and author of *Letter to God & Other Poems* (2003) and *The Bridge Selection: Poems for the Road* (2005). He lives in London with his wife and children. **Ian Badcoe** walks in the peak district and occasionally returns to the city for important supplies, such as money. **Rosemary Badcoe** has been published in a number of magazines and is undertaking an MA at Sheffield Hallam University. She is editor of the online poetry magazine *Antiphon* www.antiphon.org.uk. **R V Bailey** (the other voice in the late U A Fanthorpe's readings) is the author of *Course Work* and *Marking Time* (Peterloo Poets), *From Me to You* (with U A F, Enitharmon), and *The Losing Game* (Mariscat Press). **Bruce Barnes** is a retired charity employee, based in Bradford and working as a freelance Creative Writing facilitator and poetry-events co-ordinator. His latest collection of poetry, *Somewhere Else*, was published by Utistugu Press in 2003. **Phil Barrett** trained as an artist and is a prize-winning poet who has given readings, collaborated with composers and undertakes workshops with writing groups, individuals, and in primary and secondary schools. **Mara Bergman's** poetry has been published widely in magazines and anthologies and she is also an award-winning children's book author. She lives in Tunbridge Wells with her family. **Clare Best** lives in Lewes. Her first full collection is *Excisions* (Waterloo Press, 2011) and she is also the author of *Treasure Ground* (HappenStance, 2009). www.clarebest.co.uk. **Margaret Beston** studied foreign languages and for a while lived abroad. Her poems have appeared in several magazines and anthologies. She now lives in Kent, writing poetry and learning Japanese. **Steven Bliss** grew up in Sheffield, read English at Cambridge, and now lives near Oxford. He started writing poetry a few years ago and has, so far, had a few poems published in magazines or elsewhere. **Pat Borthwick** lives in rural East Yorkshire. She has three full-length collections and has won poetry prizes both here and abroad. She is a Creative Writing tutor and Hawthornden Fellow. **Connie Ramsay Bott** grew up in Michigan but has lived in the UK for many years. Her poems and short stories have been published in anthologies and magazines. She teaches Creative Writing. **Peter Branson's** poems have been published in magazines in Britain, the US, Canada, Eire, Australia and New Zealand, including *Acumen, Ambit, Envoi, The London Magazine, Iota, Barnwood, The Frogmore Papers, The Interpreter's House, South, Crannog* and *Other Poetry*. www.peterbranson.com. **Felicity Brookesmith** has poems in *Did I Tell You?* (WordAid), *Sixty Poems for Haiti* (Cane Arrow Press), the journal *Equinox* and collections *Trimming Up Jack* and *Tricks and Treats* (tanka/songs). **Sarah J Bryson** writes poetry and short stories. She is a founder member of Freehand (www.freehandwriters.co.uk), a writers' group which meets monthly in Oxford. **Elizabeth Burns'** most recent collection is *Held* (Polygon, 2010). Her pamphlet *The Shortest Days* won the inaugural Michael Marks Award. She lives in Lancaster. **Sue Butler** is a keen cyclist and gardener currently living in Hertfordshire, where she works as a copywriter in the weight-loss industry. **Derrick Buttress'** plays have been broadcast on BBC television and radio. Three collections of poetry have been published by Shoestring, and two memoirs. A collection of short stories is due from Shoestring. **Miki Byrne** has written two poetry collections and has read her work on TV, radio and at festivals. Over 100 anthologies and magazines have included her work and she has won 12 prizes. **Lorna Callery:** Writer/Artist/Performer/Educator/Co-Founder: Monosyllabic (www.facebook.com/pages/Monosyllabic)/Co-Founder: www.polkadotpunks.com. **Caroline Carver** has published three collections. Her work is influenced by life in Bermuda, Jamaica, Canada and now Cornwall. She won the National Poetry Prize in 1998 and was commended in 2010. **Nancy Charley** lives in Ramsgate, the south-east tip of England. She therefore loves to see things pivoting, especially through the interaction of words and people in poetry performance. **Kate Clanchy's** recent prizes include the 2009 Writers' Guild Best Book Award for *What Is She Doing Here: A Refugee Story* and the 2009 BBC National Short Story Prize for 'The Not-Dead and the Saved'. **G B Clarkson** was shortlisted for the Arvon Poetry Competition in 2010 and her poems have appeared in *Smiths Knoll, The Daily Mirror, Poetry Digest*, and (online) at *Eyewear* and *Gumbo*. **Anne Cluysenaar**, born in Belgium 1936, was brought to Britain before the last war. Publications: *Timeslips* (Carcanet, 1997), *Batu-Angas: Envisioning Nature with Alfred Russel Wallace* (Seren, 2008), *Water to Breathe* (Flarestack, 2009), *Migrations* (Cinnamon Press, 2011). At present writing a poem-diary, from which 'A Marsh Arab Returns …' is taken. **Angela Croft** worked as a journalist and her poems have recently appeared in *South, The Interpreter's House, Orbis, The French Literary Review* and *Ordinary Magic*, an anthology published by Poets Unlimited. **Martyn Crucefix's** new collection, *Hurt*, is published by Enitharmon. His translation of Rainer Maria Rilke's *Duino Elegies* (Enitharmon, 2006) was shortlisted for the 2007 Popescu Prize for European Poetry Translation.www.poetrypf.co.uk/martyncrucefixpage.html. **Abi Curtis** received an Eric Gregory Award from the Society of Authors in 2004. Her debut collection, *Unexpected Weather*, received Salt Publishing's inaugural Crashaw Prize in 2008 and was shortlisted for the London Festival Fringe poetry award 2010. **Michael Curtis:** recently returned from a residency in Béthune, he is busy working on two new collections and looking forward to reading at the Isle of Man Literature Festival in 2013. **Clare Dawes** has enjoyed teaching English as a Foreign Language for twenty-one years, but is looking forward to spending more time on her writing and her garden in the future. **Patricia Debney** wrote *Littoral Drift*, her second collection of prose poems, during a residency in a beach hut on the North Kent coast. A founding member of WordAid, she is Senior Lecturer in Creative Writing at the University of Kent. **Anna Dickie** started writing poetry in her late forties. She has two pamphlets in print: *Heart Notes* (Calder Wood Press) and *Imprint* (Jaggnath Press). **Marilyn Donovan** is one of the three poets featured in the collection *Missed Heartbeats* (Stubborn Mule, 2010). Her poem 'Scots Pine' was nominated for the Forward Single Poem Prize 2011 and she is Canterbury Poet of the Year 2011. **Barbara Dordi** edits the magazines *Equinox* and *The French Literary Review*. Her publication *Entre-Deux*, poems in English and French, is a celebration of French life. In 2009 her collection *Moving Still* was published by Cinnamon Press. She lives in France. **Val Doyle** has been writing all her life, mostly articles for various outlets, but only started writing poetry about 15 years ago. **Cath Drake**, an Australian, has been published in anthologies and poetry magazines in the UK, Australia and the US. She performs her work, runs writing workshops, and her background in non-fiction includes award-winning journalism. http://cathdrake.wordpress.com. **Margaret Eddershaw:** poet-performer, with a background in theatre and more recently in poetry, mostly inspired by living in Greece and travel to forty countries in the last fifteen years. **Catherine Edmunds** is a writer/artist, best known for her solo poetry collection *wormwood, earth and honey*, novel *Small Poisons* (both Circaidy Gregory Press) and illustrations for BeWrite Books et al. **June English** has published three volumes of poetry: "You should read these poems for their strange insight into human nature, and for their shocking accuracy in revealing it." (U A Fanthorpe and R V Bailey). **Simon Everett** holds an MA in Creative Writing from the University of Kent; he was winner of the 2010 UKC T S Eliot Prize and was shortlisted again in 2011. **Jo Field's** small collection *The Space Beyond* is a WordAid publication raising money for Dementia UK. **Janice Fixter's** last collection, *a kind of slow motion*, was published in 2007. **Kate L Fox** enjoys reading and writing poetry. She has an MA in Creative Writing from the University of Kent and has had some of her prose poems published. Poems that mix humour, lyricism and everyday observations are what she strives to achieve! **Wendy French** has two collections of poetry published: *Splintering the Dark* (Rockingham Press) and *Surely You Know This* (Tall-lighthouse Press, 2009). This title is one of Sappho's fragments. **Dorothy Fryd** teaches Creative Writing for the University of Kent. She has been published in *The Rialto*, *BRAND Magazine*, *Obsessed With Pipework*, *The Interpreter's House* and *South Bank Poetry Magazine*. **Anne-Marie Fyfe's** latest collection is *Understudies: New and Selected Poems* (Seren, 2010). She runs the Coffee-House Poetry reading series at London's Troubadour Coffee-House and was chair of the Poetry Society from 2007 to 2010. **Nancy Gaffield** lectures at the University of Kent. Her first book *Tokaido Road* (CB Editions) was a Poetry Book Society recommendation and was shortlisted for the Forward First Collection Prize. **Katherine Gallagher** is a widely published Australian-born poet resident in North London. She has five full-length collections of poetry, most recently *Carnival Edge: New & Selected Poems* (Arc Publications, 2010). www.katherine-gallagher.com. **Victoria Gatehouse** has an MA in Creative Writing from Manchester Metropolitan University. Her poetry has been published in a number of well-respected magazines and shortlisted in various competitions. **Vanessa Gebbie** www.vanessagebbie.com. **Alan Gleave** is a retired teacher. He has Deal Writers to thank for finding renewed creative impetus, and has had poems published in various magazines including *The Reader* and *The Interpreter's House*. **Daphne Gloag** was a medical editor and journalist. Her second collection was *A Compression of Distances* (Cinnamon Press, 2009). Awards include first prizes in Poetry on the Lake and *Scintilla* competitions. **Rebecca Goss** lives in Liverpool. Her poems have appeared in many literary journals and anthologies. Her first full-length collection is *The Anatomy of Structures* (Flambard Press, 2010). **Nicky Gould** is a founder member of WordAid and is currently studying for an MA in Creative Writing at the University of Kent. Her poetry can be found in various publications and anthologies. **John Greening's** next collection, *To the War Poets*, is from Oxford Poets. He is winner of a Cholmondeley Award and the Bridport Prize. His *Poetry Masterclass* appeared recently. **Patricia Griffin** has been writing poetry for eight years. She lives in Whitstable and enjoys walking and gardening. **David Grubb** has a new poetry collection due from Shearsman Books, and a short story collection will be published by Leaf Books. He founded Children's Aid Direct. **Duncan Hall** lives in Bolton. chasic@hotmail.co.uk. **Robert Hamberger** has been awarded a Hawthornden Fellowship and shortlisted for a Forward Prize. His collections are *Warpaint Angel* (1997), *The Smug Bridegroom* (2002) and *Torso* (Redbeck Press, 2007). **Maggie Harris** has published five collections of poetry and a memoir, *Kiskadee Girl* (Kingston University Press, 2011). She has won many awards for her poetry and fiction. In 2011–12 she is touring *Daughters*, a poetry, music and dance collaboration with five other Kent artists. **David Harsent** has published ten volumes of poetry. *Legion* won the Forward Best Collection Prize 2005; *Night* was published in 2011 and has been shortlisted for the T S Eliot Award and Forward Prize. **Christopher Hobday** was born in Preston in 1979. He is assistant editor of the *Conversation Paperpress*. His poetry has appeared in volumes including *Stubborn Mule Orchestra* alongside two fellow poets and *Adage Adagio*, a dialogue poem with David Nettleingham. **Mark Holihan**, a writer and multi-media artist, is a former Californian now transplanted to Kent. **Jamie A Hughes** is a French horn playing, baseball loving, cat rearing, former English teacher turned copy/content editor living in Atlanta, Georgia. She believes soli Deo Gloria in all things! **Sandra Ireland** is a mature student, with one poem published previously. She lives in Carnoustie, Scotland, in a tiny cottage by the sea which should be inspirational, but is actually just messy. **Stephen Ireland** lives in London. He is studying for an MA in Creative Writing at the University of Kent and is currently working on a novel. **Andy Jackson** is from Manchester but now lives in Scotland. His poems have been published in *Magma*, *Poetry News* and on the walls of public conveniences in the Shetland Islands. His collection *The Assassination Museum* was published by Red Squirrel Press in 2010. www.soutarwriters.co.uk/andyjackson. **Sarah James** is a prize-winning journalist, fiction writer and poet. Her poetry collection *Into the Yell* (Circaidy Gregory Press, 2010) won third prize in the International Rubery Book Award 2011.www.sarah-james.co.uk. **Maria Jastrzębska** was born in Warsaw, Poland. Recent collections include *Syrena* (Redback Press, 2004), *I'll Be Back Before You Know It* (Pighog Press) and *Everyday Angels* (Waterloo Press, 2009). **Ben Johnson** lives in the New Forest where he likes to read poetry in the garden. In his spare time he enjoys juggling with words. **Anne-Marie Jordan:** Crumpled receipts rescued from coat pockets, backs of battered bus tickets + envelopes ripped open collaborate under the auspices of AMJ's poetry incubator. One day, a notebook will be hers… **Jenifer Kahawatte** studied Creative Writing at the University of Kent. Now retired from full-time work,

she writes for pleasure. She was a runner-up in the Bridport Poetry Prize 2008. **Meena Kandasamy** is a writer, poet and activist based in India. She has published two collections of poetry: *Touch* (2006) and *Ms Militancy* (2010). **Ann Kelley's** novel *Bowerbird* (Luath Press) won the Costa Book of the Year 2007 (Children's Category). Poetry collections: *Paper Whites* (LME), *Because We Have Reached That Place* (Oversteps Books), *Raining Cats and Dogs* (Oversteps Books). www.annkelley.co.uk. **Anne Kenny** began writing poetry while living in Melbourne, Australia, during 2003. Her poems have been published in *Blue Dog: Australian Poetry*, *Equinox*, *South* and *Mirror Writing* by common room poets. **Mimi Khalvati** has published seven collections with Carcanet Press, including *The Meanest Flower*, shortlisted for the T S Eliot Prize, and *Child: New & Selected Poems*, a Poetry Book Society Special Commendation. **John Killick** is based in West Yorkshire. His most recent publication (with Myra Schneider) is *Writing Your Self*. He publishes poems, essays and criticism regularly in *The North*. **Jane Kirwan** has two poetry collections, *Stealing the Eiffel Tower* (1997) and *The Man Who Sold Mirrors* (2003). She won an Arts Council Writers Award, 2002. *Second Exile* (Rockingham Press, 2010, Novela Bohemica, 2011) is a poem/prose memoir of her Czech partner. **Wendy Klein** was born in the United States and came to Britain in 1971. A retired psychotherapist, she is published in magazines and anthologies. Her first collection, *Cuba in the Blood*, was published by Cinnamon Press in 2009. **Frances Knight** is a musician and composer. She also writes poetry and prose and was shortlisted for the Bridport Short Story Prize 2010. She is currently working on a new album with her band 'My Dream Kitchen'…
Gillian Laker was born in Hong Kong and currently lives in Kent. Her poems have been published in various anthologies and included in an international multi-media exhibition in Odense, Denmark. **Michael Laskey** co-founded the Aldeburgh Poetry Festival and edits the poetry magazine *Smiths Knoll*. He has published four collections, most recently *The Man Alone: New and Selected Poems* (2008). **Mark Leech's** poems appear in the Bloodaxe Books anthology *Voice Recognition*. His long poem sequence *London Water* was published by Flarestack in 2008. He lives in Oxford. **Bob Le Vaillant** was a social worker in East London, following a full career in the Army. Living now in Deal, Kent, he is a magistrate, school governor and dad to three teenagers. **Richard Lung** has a flood poem and others in *Kritya* (online). He also has poems in *Star*line*, as well as SF acceptances for *Dark Metre* and *Kaleidotrope*. **John Lyons** has five published poetry collections, and *Cook-Up in a Trini Kitchen*, a collection of poems, recipes, drawings and watercolours. He performs at literature festivals, and on radio and television. **John Mackay** is doing a PhD on contemporary American elegy

at Birkbeck College, London. **Luigi Marchini** was brought up in London in the 20th century where he spent many a happy maths and physics lesson at the National Film Theatre. **Andrew McCallum** lives in Biggar, South Lanarkshire, with his wife and three children and works for a small charity in Edinburgh. He makes poetry in his spare time. **Maria C McCarthy's** poetry collection *strange fruits* is published by WordAid to raise funds for Macmillan Cancer Support. www.medwaymaria.co.uk. **Gill McEvoy:** Two pamphlets from Happenstance Press (*Uncertain Days*, 2006 and *A Sampler*, 2008). Full collection *The Plucking Shed* (Cinnamon Press, 2010). **Joan Michelson**, Londoner, teaches poetry at Birkbeck College and in the community. Her collection treating loss and recovery, *Toward the Heliopause* (Poetic Matrix Publishers, US, 2011), can be ordered from Amazon. **Janet Montefiore**, Professor of 20th Century English Literature at Kent University, wrote *Feminism and Poetry* (1987, 2004) and *Rudyard Kipling* (2007). Her poems have appeared in numerous journals and anthologies. **Christopher R Moore** is a writer of confessional poetry and prose. He is also a George Eliot apologist, a Scotch Whisky enthusiast and a semi-professional wrestler. **Hubert Moore's** sixth collection, *The Hearing Room* (Shoestring, 2006), has recently been republished. His next collection, *A Garment of Two Greens*, is due from Shoestring in spring 2012. **Richard Moorhead** has had poetry published in *Anon*, *Mimesis*, *The Horizon Review* and *The Financial Times*. His pamphlet *The Reluctant Vegetarian* (Oystercatcher Press) was shortlisted for the Michael Marks Award. **Esther Morgan** has published three collections of poetry with Bloodaxe Books; the most recent, *Grace* (2011), is a Poetry Book Society Recommendation. She lives in Norfolk with her husband and new daughter. **Abegail Morley's** collection *How to Pour Madness into a Teacup* was shortlisted for the Forward Best First Collection Prize. She is guest poetry editor at *The New Writer*. **Valerie Morton** has had her poetry published by Leaf Books, *The New Writer*, Indigo Dreams and *The Guardian* online. She lives in Hertfordshire and runs a Creative Writing workshop with a mental health charity. **Cheryl Moskowitz:** Co-founder of LAPIDUS, tutor at Sussex University (1996–2010). Prizewinner in 2010 Bridport and Troubadour Poetry Competitions and the 2011 Hippocrates Prize for Poetry and Medicine. Novel, *Wyoming Trail* (Granta, 1998). **Elly Niland** is a Guyanese teacher, poet and playwright. Her first collection, *In Retrospect*, was runner-up for the Guyana Prize. Her second, *Cornerstones*, was winner of the Guyana Prize for Literature 2006. Forthcoming: short stories supported by Arts Council England. **Elly Nobbs** lives in Prince Edward Island, Canada. She's had poems published by *The New Writer*. **Ruth O'Callaghan:** Hawthornden Fellow, tutor, mentor, reviewer, interviewer, adjudicator. Hosts two poetry venues, translated into six languages, has read extensively worldwide, awarded Arts Council grant to work in Mongolia, a gold medal in Taiwan; has three full collections. **John O'Donoghue** is the author of *Sectioned: A Life Interrupted*. His memoir recounts his life in and out of asylums, homeless hostels, and prison. It was awarded Mind Book of the Year 2010. **Alice Oswald** won the Forward Prize 1996 with *The Thing in the Gap-Stone Stile*, the T S Eliot Award with *Dart* (Faber), the Geoffrey Faber Memorial Prize 2006 with *Woods, Etc.*, the inaugural Ted Hughes Award with *Weeds and Wild Flowers*, and a Cholmondeley Award in 2009 for her contribution to poetry. **Fiona Owen's** poetry collections include *Going Gentle* and *Imagining the Full Hundred*. A new collection, co-written with Meredith Andrea, is forthcoming, published by Cinnamon Press. Fiona teaches for the Open University and lives in Wales. **Jeremy Page** published *In and Out of the Dark Wood* with HappenStance in 2010 and his translations from Catullus were published in June 2011. He lives in Lewes. **Geraldine Paine** is an award-winning poet who has been published widely in magazines and anthologies. Her first collection, *The Go-Away-Bird*, was published by Lapwing Publications (Belfast) in 2008. **Pascale Petit's** latest collection is *What the Water Gave Me: Poems after Frida Kahlo* (Seren, 2010); it was shortlisted for the T S Eliot Prize and Wales Book of the Year, and was a book of the year in *The Observer*. **Mario Petrucci**, ecologist, physicist and Royal Literary Fund Fellow, is a multi-award-winning poet and literary frontiersman. His acclaimed book and film concerning the survivors and casualties of Chernobyl, both entitled *Heavy Water*, are available via www.mariopetrucci.com. **Katrina Porteous'** long poems for BBC Radio include: *Horse*, *The Refuge Box*, *Dunstanburgh* and *Longshore Drift*. Her books include *The Lost Music* (Bloodaxe Books, 1996) and *The Blue Lonnen* (Jardine, 2007). **Derrick Porter** has been published in numerous magazines such as *Acumen*, *Magma* and *The Long Poem* and in several anthologies including *I Am Twenty People* (Enitharmon) and *this little stretch of life* (Hearing Eye). **Kyrill Potapov** is originally from Moscow. He is an English teacher who seizes breaktimes to work on his novel. **Caroline Price** works as a violinist and teacher in Tunbridge Wells, where she also helps to run the Kent & Sussex Poetry Society. Her third collection of poetry, *Wishbone*, was published by Shoestring in 2008. **Harriet Proudfoot** was a primary teacher. Her interests include writing, drawing, movement and theatre, and her chapter published in *Development through the Creative Arts*. Now she enjoys teaching poetry with adults. **Lynne Rees** is a Welsh writer, editor and tutor living in Kent. www.lynneress.com. **Jean Rees-Lyons** writes full-time; holds a Post-Graduate Diploma in Community Theatre; has published poems in winners' anthologies; develops new dramatic poetry and prose with creative professionals and non-professionals in Cambridgeshire. **Mary Robinson** is a writer and adult education tutor living in Cumbria. Her collection *The Art of Gardening* was published by Flambard Press in 2010. She blogs at http://maryrobinsonpoetry.blogspot.com. **Mark Roper's** most recent publications are *Even So: New & Selected Poems* (Dedalus Press, 2008) and *The River Book: A Celebration of the Suir*, a collaboration with the photographer Paddy Dwan (Whimbrel Press, 2010). **Sue Rose** was born in London, now lives in Kent where she works as a literary translator. She won the Troubadour Poetry Prize in 2009 and the Canterbury Poet of the Year competition in 2008. Her debut collection, *From the Dark Room*, is published by Cinnamon Press (2011). **Lucy Rutter** enjoys collaborative writing, often working with visual artists. A really exciting shared energy often emerges. She also works as a teacher, delivering outreach programmes for the University of Kent. **Carole Satyamurti:** A new collection, *Countdown*, was published by Bloodaxe Books in June 2011. **Natalie Savage** is still enthralled by the haiku form: a place to say so much in just a breath. **Maggie Sawkins** organises Tongues & Grooves Poetry and Music Club in Portsmouth. She runs Creative Writing projects in community and healthcare settings and is a tutor for The Poetry School. www.maggiesawkins.com. **Mary Scheurer** was educated in Manchester and Liverpool. She now teaches English and Philosophy in Switzerland. Her poems and short stories have been published in both Britain and Europe. **Myra Schneider's** recent books are *Circling The Core* (Enitharmon, 2008) and the resource book *Writing Your Self* (Continuum, 2009) with John Killick. She is consultant to the Second Light Network. **Derek Score** was born in 1931 and began to write when he retired from teaching. One collection, *The Dark Sargasso Sea*. Another one due soon. **Derek Sellen** lives and teaches in Canterbury. His poetry has been published widely. Most recently, the sequence 'A Guide to the Spanish Painters' has been published in *Kaleidoscope* (Cinnamon Press). **Bernard Sharratt** was born in Liverpool in 1944; taught at University of Kent, etc; retired, gladly. **Penelope Shuttle's** tenth poetry collection is *Sandgrain and Hourglass* (Bloodaxe Books, 2010). **John Siddique** is author of *Full Blood, Recital – An Almanac, Poems From A Northern Soul* and *The Prize*. *The Prize* was nominated for the Forward Prize and his children's book *Don't Wear It On Your Head* was shortlisted for the CLPE Poetry Award. www.johnsiddique.co.uk. **silent lotus** is a spiritual advisor. His poetry has been published in Europe, England, America and Canada. He resides in The Netherlands and America with the artist Nermin Kura. www.silentlotus.net. **Fiona Sinclair's** work has appeared in numerous publications. Her second collection, *A Game of Hide* *and Seek*, will be published in late 2011 by Indigo Dreams. She is the editor of the online poetry magazine *Message in a Bottle*. **Catherine Smith** writes poetry and fiction. She teaches for the University of Sussex, The Poetry School and the Arvon Foundation. Her latest collection, *Lip* (Smith/Doorstop), was shortlisted for the Forward Prize. **Rupert Smith** is an award-winning poet. After completing a Creative Writing MA at Kent, he plans to train to teach secondary English and to secretly overload the curriculum with poetry. **Ruth Smith** first took up writing when she retired from teaching and since then, with a lot of help from some very talented tutors, she has had poems published in various magazines and anthologies. **Simon Smith** has published four collections of poems; the latest is *London Bridge* (2010). He translates poems from French and Latin, and lectures in Creative Writing at the University of Kent. **Colin Speakman** lives in Ilkley, West Yorkshire. He is best known as the author of several books about walking and the Yorkshire Dales and as the founder of the Yorkshire Dales Society. **Anne Stewart's** first collection is *The Janus Hour* (Oversteps Books, 2010). She has an MA (Dist.) in Creative Writing from Sheffield Hallam University and she won the Bridport Prize in 2008. **Michael Stewart** is a multi-award winning writer based in Bradford. His debut novel *King Crow* has just been shortlisted for the Not-the-Booker prize. www.michael-stewart.org.uk. **Wisty Thomas's** poems have been published in various magazines, including *Envoi, South, Equinox, The Interpreter's House* and *South Bank Poetry*. She is one of the poets in the anthology *Ordinary Magic*. **Moyra Tourlamain** was Canterbury Festival Poet of the Year 2010/11 and was shortlisted for the University of Kent's 2011 T S Eliot Prize. She has been a publisher, magazine editor, broadcaster, and BBC bureaucrat. **Deborah Trayhurn's** poems appear in many competition anthologies, including Bridport, Manchester Cathedral International (First Prize), New Writing Scotland, and Cinnamon Press. Her pamphlet collection *Embracing Water* is published by Happenstance. **Michael James Treacy** fancies himself a writer and claims that poetry is the vocabulary of his heart, soul, mind, gut and occasionally his rear end. **Vivienne Tregenza** is a Cornish poet. She has lived in Malaya, Borneo, Sri Lanka, Turkey and France, but happily returned to her roots in Penwith, where she lives with her family. **Vincent Turner** lives in Donegal, Ireland. His works have appeared in various 'zines on the web and his first chapbook, *Envying Harry*, was published in 2009. He is currently working towards publication of his second chapbook. **Sindonia Tyrell** lives in Deal, is a member of the Bellyfuls, and writes poetry which very occasionally gets published somewhere (much to her delight!). **Eleanor J Vale** lives near Cambridge. Her poems have been published in magazines including *Smiths Knoll*, *The Interpreter's House*, *The New Writer* and *Mslexia*. **Eleanor Ward** recently completed an undergraduate degree at the University of Kent and is now studying for an MSc in Medical Humanities at Kings College London, but continues to write every day! **Rory Waterman** lives in Bristol. His poems have appeared in the *Times Literary Supplement*, *Agenda*, *PN Review*, *Stand* and elsewhere, and a selection is forthcoming in *New Poetries V* (Carcanet, 2011). He is working on a first collection. **Megan Watkins** lives in London and her poetry has been published in recent editions of *Sentinel Literary Quarterly*, *Rhino Poetry*, *Gloom Cupboard*, *The Journal* and *Fourteen Magazine*. She also participated in WordAid's first anthology. **Christine West** was born and educated in London. Her poems and stories have appeared in poetry reviews, an American anthology, and a book about her husband's childhood. **Linda White** has won prizes for her poetry and been published in *Mslexia*, *Equinox* and *South Bank Poetry*. Her work was included in the anthology *Ordinary Magic*. **Catherine Whittaker** has been published in many anthologies and magazines, and was the Poet Laureate of Warwick (2008/9). She tutors in Poetry and Life Writing for Warwick University and runs courses and workshops in Creative Writing with a colleague, www.openmindwriting.com. **Susan Wicks'** latest collection, *House of Tongues*, is a Poetry Book Society Recommendation. Her translation of Valerie Rouzeau, *Cold Spring in Winter*, won the Scott-Moncrieff Prize and was shortlisted for Canada's international Griffin Prize for Poetry. **Vicky Wilson** is a poet, journalist, editor, publisher, performer and educator. Her poetry has been widely published and her book *London's Houses* is available from www.metropublications.com. **Rachel Woolf** has been placed in poetry competitions and published in *Did I Tell You?*, *New Writing Scotland*, *qzrrtsiluni* and a National Galleries of Scotland anthology.

ACKNOWLEDGEMENTS

Shanta Acharya 'Survival' was previously published in her collection *Looking In, Looking Out* (Headland Publications, 2005). **Patience Agbabi** 'The Wife of Bafa' was first published in *Transformatrix* (Canongate Books, 2000). **Moira Andrew** 'The old story' was first published in her second collection, *Fresh Out of Dragonflies* (Headlock Press, 1995). **R V Bailey** 'Suddenly' was first published in *The North* magazine. **Bruce Barnes** 'The Economy of Sweets' was first published in his collection *The Lovelife of the Absent Minded* (Phoenix Press, 1993). **Clare Best** 'Self-portrait without breasts' was previously published in *Poetry News*, winter 2008/09, *Of Love and Hope* (Avalanche Books, 2010) and *Excisions* (Waterloo Press, 2011). **Margaret Beston** 'Hibaku' was first published in *The New Writer*, then in the anthology *Ordinary Magic* in June 2011. **Peter Branson** 'Swifts' was first published in *Nap Magazine*. **Felicity Brookesmith** 'Teeth' is in her collection *Trimming Up Jack*, raising funds for Breast Cancer Campaign. **Elizabeth Burns'** 'A language of flowers' was first published in *Held* (Poylygon, 2010). **Sue Butler** 'Germination' won a small prize in The Cardiff Poetry Competition a number of years ago. **Derrick Buttress** 'Reading The Weather' was first published in the collection *Destinations* (Shoestring, 2009). **Kate Clanchy** 'Ararat' was first published in *Newborn* (Picador, 2004). **Abi Curtis** 'Death by Lightning' was first published in *Unexpected Weather* (Salt, 2011). **Anna Dickie** 'Snow' received a special merit award in the National Galleries of Scotland 2011 'Inspired? Get writing' competition, and is in her pamphlet *Imprint* (Jaggnath Press). **Marilyn Donovan** 'Scots Pine' was published in *Dream Catcher 24*. **June English** 'Between Worlds' was published in her collection *Sunflower Equations* (Hearing Eye, 2008). **Wendy French** 'The Doctor's Wife' won second prize in the 2011 Hippocrates Poetry & Medicine Prize. **Anne-Marie Fyfe** 'Interstate' was published in *Understudies: New and Selected Poems* (Seren, 2010). **Katherine Gallagher** 'The Year of the Tree' appeared in *Circus-Apprentice* (Arc Publications, 2006) and later in *Carnival Edge: New & Selected Poems* (Arc Publications, 2010). **Daphne Gloag** 'Not Only Dark' was published in *Kaleidoscope: An Anthology of Poetry Sequences* (Cinnamon Press, 2011) and is part of 'Black Hole and Ring of Light', which is one section of a long poem entitled *Beginnings*. **Robert Hamberger** 'Fox and Deer' was originally published in *Torso* (Redbeck Press, 2007). **David Harsent** 'Metals with a Memory…' was first published in *Discourses – Poems for the Royal Institution* edited by Jo Shapcott and published by the Calouste Gulbenkian Foundation. **Sarah James** 'Unsubmerged' was first published in her collection *Into the Yell* (Circaidy Gregory Press, 2010).

Maria Jastrzębska A version of 'Your Father, Leonard…' was first featured in *I'll Be Back Before You Know It* (Pighog Press, 2009). **Ann Kelley** 'Flaming Stargazer' won Second Prize in the 2011 Torriano Poetry Competition. **Mimi Khalvati** 'The Blanket' was first published in *Poetry Review*, Vol 101:2 Summer 2011. **John Killick** 'The Descent of K2' appeared in a pamphlet from Smith/ Doorstop Books entitled *Singular Persons*. **Frances Knight** 'The Stone' was first published in *Circled Like a Target* (2004). **Michael Laskey** 'Permission to Breathe' is taken from his collection *Permission to Breathe* (Smith/Doorstop Books). **John Lyons** 'Lougaroo's Survival' is revised from *Behind The Carnival* (Smith/Doorstop Books). **Luigi Marchini** 'Outlaw' was first published in *Stubborn Mule Orchestra* (2008). **Maria C McCarthy** 'Survival' was first published in *Night Train 4* (University of Kent, 2006) and also appears in *strange fruits* (2011). **Gill McEvoy** 'Surviving' was first published on the *ink sweat and tears* poetry website. **Esther Morgan** 'Why don't you just leave?' was first published in her collection *The Silence Living in Houses* (Bloodaxe Books, 2005). **Cheryl Moskowitz** 'Moving the Stag Head to Aunt Irma's' was inspired by photographs and quotations from the book *Family* (Twin Palms Publishers, 2010), courtesy of Chris Verene. **Elly Niland** 'Light' is taken from her third collection, *East of Centre* (Dido Press, 2008). **Ruth O'Callaghan** 'When you say Dance? …' was first published in *Where Acid Has Etched* (bluechrome, 2007). **Alice Oswald** 'Bristly Ox-tongue' was published in *Weeds and Wild Flowers*, with etchings by Jessica Greenman (Faber, 2009). **Fiona Owen** 'The Dog Shoot' was published in her book *Imagining the Full Hundred* (Gwasg Pantycelyn, 2003). **Pascale Petit** 'Remembrance of an Open Wound' was published in *What the Water Gave Me: Poems after Frida Kahlo* (Seren, 2010). **Mario Petrucci** 'Orders of Magnitude' was first published in *Flowers of Sulphur* (Enitharmon, 2007) and formed part of 'Poetry: The Environment, a resource pack for teachers of creative writing'. **Katrina Porteous** 'Snail' is an excerpt from *Dunstanburgh* (Smokestack, 2004). This radio poem was first commissioned by BBC Radio 4 and broadcast in 2004, produced by Julian May. **Caroline Price** 'Pneumonia' was first published in *The Interpreter's House* in 2003, then in her collection *Wishbone* (2008). **Lynne Rees** 'Deep' was first published in *The Rialto*, May 2005. **Mary Robinson** 'Age' was included in the Climate Change Exhibition held at the Neo Gallery in Cockermouth in July 2007. **Sue Rose** 'Mahler 9' won the Troubadour Poetry Prize in 2009 and was featured on the Coffee House website for the year. It is also published in her book, *From the Dark Room* (Cinnamon Press, 2011). **Carole Satyamurti** 'How I Altered History' was first published in *Ambit*, and is included in her *Stitching the Dark: new and selected poems* (Bloodaxe Books, 2005). **Maggie Sawkins** 'The Birds' won first prize in the 18th Annual Writers Conference Poetry Competition and was published in *The Zig Zag Woman* (Two Ravens Press, 2007). **Myra Schneider** 'The Car' was first published in *Multiplying the Moon* (Enitharmon, 2004). **Derek Sellen** 'Standing with Oliver in Oliver's Garden' was first published in the *Sentinel Annual Literature Anthology* (2011). **John Siddique** 'Thirst' was first published in *Full Blood* (Salt, 2011). **Fiona Sinclair** 'Day Tripper' was previously published in *The Jest Fuel Review* and *A Game of Hide and Seek (*Indigo Dreams). **Ruth Smith** 'Khaki' was first published online when it won the Wells Poetry Competition a few years ago. **Simon Smith** 'Poem 8' is taken from *PN Review* 148, Volume 29, Number 2, November/December 2002. Original poem by Roman poet Catullus. **Colin Speakman** 'At St David's' has just been published in *Dune Fox and Other Poems* (Fighting Cock Press). **Anne Stewart** 'The Meeting of Generous-Seeming Men' is published in her collection *The Janus Hour* (Oversteps Books, 2010). **Vivienne Tregenza** 'Reef' was first published in *The Sunday Observer*, Sri Lanka, 3 February 2008. **Eleanor J Vale** 'The Last Photo' was published in *Mslexia* in 2006. **Eleanor Ward** 'Sea' was first published in *New Forum* (UCI Undergraduate Creative Writing, Fall 2009, Volume 12, Issue 3). **Rory Waterman** 'Back' was first published in *Able Muse Review*. **Megan Watkins** 'The imagined woman can't defend herself' was first published in *The Journal*. Susan Wicks 'Nuclear' was published in *House of Tongues*, 2011, and is reproduced by kind permission of Bloodaxe Books. **Vicky Wilson** 'Visiting Grimes Graves' forms part of the touring show 'Daughters'. **Rachel Woolf** 'And Cradled It' appeared in English and Scots in *New Writing Scotland 29*.

Lightning Source UK Ltd.
Milton Keynes UK
UKOW051006091111

181736UK00001B/5/P